# TEACHER'S PET PUBLICATIONS

## LITPLAN TEACHER PACK
for
Treasure Island
based on the book by
Robert Louis Stevenson

Written by
Mary B. Collins

© 1996 Teacher's Pet Publications
All Rights Reserved

This **LitPlan** for Robert Louis Stevenson's
*Treasure Island*
has been brought to you by Teacher's Pet Publications, Inc.

Copyright Teacher's Pet Publications 1996
11504 Hammock Point
Berlin MD 21811

Only the student materials in this unit plan (such as worksheets, study questions, and tests) may be reproduced multiple times for use in the purchaser's classroom.

For any additional copyright questions,
contact Teacher's Pet Publications.

www.tpet.com

# TABLE OF CONTENTS - *Treasure Island*

| | |
|---|---|
| Introduction | 6 |
| Unit Objectives | 8 |
| Reading Assignment Sheet | 9 |
| Unit Outline | 10 |
| Study Questions (Short Answer) | 13 |
| Quiz/Study Questions (Multiple Choice) | 19 |
| Pre-reading Vocabulary Worksheets | 33 |
| Lesson One (Introductory Lesson) | 49 |
| Nonfiction Assignment Sheet | 51 |
| Oral Reading Evaluation Form | 53 |
| Writing Assignment 1 | 59 |
| Writing Assignment 2 | 65 |
| Writing Assignment 3 | 68 |
| Writing Evaluation Form | 67 |
| Vocabulary Review Activities | 63 |
| Extra Writing Assignments/Discussion ?s | 61 |
| Unit Review Activities | 70 |
| Unit Tests | 73 |
| Unit Resource Materials | 103 |
| Vocabulary Resource Materials | 117 |

# A FEW NOTES ABOUT THE AUTHOR
## Robert Louis Stevenson

STEVENSON, Robert Louis (1850-1894). The history of English literature records no braver story than the life and work of Robert Louis Stevenson. He was a happy and gifted storyteller, poet, and essayist. Stevenson was born Nov. 13, 1850, in Edinburgh, Scotland. He spent much of his childhood in bed, always ill with lung trouble. He died at the early age of 44. Nevertheless, in 20 years he produced an enormous quantity of work of enduring quality. He did not allow his pain and weakness to affect his gaiety or his imaginative writing.

While shut away from ordinary childish pleasures, Stevenson wrote his autobiographical poems, 'A Child's Garden of Verses'. In these he created a wonderful world of romance out of the simplest things. He did not grow weary of his bed or resent it as a substitute for happy living. It was "the pleasant land of counterpane." His mother read to him the stories which he loved to hear. He began to compose stories when he was six years old by dictating his ideas. Meanwhile his devoted Scottish nurse Alison Cunningham kept him alive by her constant care.

No regular schoolwork was possible in his childhood. He lived much of the time in a beautiful country home. Sometimes he took journeys with his father, a civil engineer, inspecting lighthouses and harbors about the wild coast. His mind became filled with images of mountain, moor, and seagirt isles.

When he grew older, he was able to take courses in Edinburgh University and to study engineering. It became plain, however, that he could not stand the activity of an engineer's life. He studied law and was admitted to the bar in 1875; but he had no liking for law. He decided to develop his natural gift for speech and writing.

While spending the winter of 1873-74 on the Riviera, because of a severe spell of bad health, he began contributing essays to periodicals. Even in these early works he showed ability to write in a charming, easy style. In 1874 he joined the Saville Club in London and made friends among leading literary men.

After being admitted to the bar, he spent several years wandering through France, Germany, and Scotland for his health. These journeys were recorded in 'An Inland Voyage' in 1878 and 'Travels with a Donkey' in 1879. Readers were charmed by Stevenson's delightful conversational manner and by the graceful flow of his style. They did not realize how hard a schooling he had given himself in the art of writing.

All his life he labored for perfection in his writing. With the publication of his first long tale, 'Treasure Island', in 1883, Stevenson became widely popular. He wrote many essays, poems, and short stories, and then in 1886 another absorbing story of adventure, 'Kidnapped'. Stevenson did not concern himself with the problems of life and society, the mysteries of thought and conduct into which George Eliot and Thomas Hardy and other realists of the 19th century delved so deeply. He returned to the pure romanticism of Scott-the love of a story for its own sake, the delight in adventure, the spirit of eternal youth.

The great romance of Stevenson's life began in France in 1876, when he met Mrs. Fanny de Grift Osbourne. Stevenson knew immediately that she was the one woman for him. But there were many difficulties. She returned to her home in San Francisco and Stevenson, hearing that she was ill, decided to follow her. He crossed the Atlantic in the steerage and the continent in an immigrant train. The experience gave him material for several books but, together with the hard times he suffered in San Francisco, nearly killed him. He developed tuberculosis and would have died had it not been for Mrs. Osbourne, who nursed him back to health. In 1880 they were married, and Stevenson returned with his wife and stepchildren to Scotland.

Stevenson could not stand the severe climate of Scotland and so for years he wandered from place to place in search of a climate where he might live and work. After an extended South Sea Island cruise he settled at last with his family in one of the Samoan Islands (Upolu) in the South Pacific, where he bought a large estate. He took a great interest in Samoan affairs and was beloved by the natives, who called him "Tusitala" (teller of tales). The end of his brave struggle came suddenly on Dec. 3, 1894. While talking gaily on the veranda of his house at Vailima he had a stroke of apoplexy and died within a few hours. The natives carried his body to Mount Vaea, cutting a path to the summit with their knives and axes. There they buried him and there he lies today in a windswept solitude overlooking the Pacific, with one of his brave verses for an epitaph:

> Under the wide and starry sky,
> Dig the grave and let me lie.
> Glad did I live, and gladly die,
> And I laid me down with a will.
> This be the verse you grave for me:
> "Here he lies where he longed to be.
> Home is the sailor, home from the sea,
> And the hunter home from the hill."

Stevenson's best-known works are: 'An Inland Voyage' (1878); 'Travels with a Donkey' (1879); 'Virginibus Puerisque' (1881); 'Familiar Studies of Men and Books' (1882); 'New Arabian Nights' (1882); 'The Silverado Squatters' (1883); 'A Child's Garden of Verses' (1885); 'Prince Otto' (1885); 'The Strange Case of Dr. Jekyll and Mr. Hyde' (1886); 'Kidnapped' (1886); 'The Merry Men and Other Tales' including 'Markheim' (1887); 'Underwoods' (1887); 'Memories and Portraits' (1887); 'The Wrong Box' (1888); 'The Master of Ballantrae' (1889); 'The Wrecker' (1892); 'The Ebb Tide' (1893); 'Catriona' (1893); 'David Balfour' (1893); 'Weir of Hermiston' (unfinished).

--- Courtesy of Compton's Learning Company

# INTRODUCTION

This unit has been designed to develop students' reading, writing, thinking, and language skills through exercises and activities related to *Treasure Island* by Robert Louis Stevenson. It includes eighteen lessons, supported by extra resource materials.

The **introductory lesson** introduces students to one main idea in the novel through a bulletin board activity. Following the introductory activity, students are given a transition to explain how the activity relates to the book they are about to read. Following the transition, students are given the materials they will be using during the unit. At the end of the lesson, students begin the pre-reading work for the first reading assignment.

The **reading assignments** are approximately thirty pages each; some are a little shorter while others are a little longer. Students have approximately 15 minutes of pre-reading work to do prior to each reading assignment. This pre-reading work involves reviewing the study questions for the assignment and doing some vocabulary work for 8 to 10 vocabulary words they will encounter in their reading.

The **study guide questions** are fact-based questions; students can find the answers to these questions right in the text. These questions come in two formats: short answer or multiple choice. The best use of these materials is probably to use the short answer version of the questions as study guides for students (since answers will be more complete), and to use the multiple choice version for occasional quizzes. It might be a good idea to make transparencies of your answer keys for the overhead projector.

The **vocabulary work** is intended to enrich students' vocabularies as well as to aid in the students' understanding of the book. Prior to each reading assignment, students will complete a two-part worksheet for approximately 8 to 10 vocabulary words in the upcoming reading assignment. Part I focuses on students' use of general knowledge and contextual clues by giving the sentence in which the word appears in the text. Students are then to write down what they think the words mean based on the words' usage. Part II nails down the definitions of the words by giving students dictionary definitions of the words and having students match the words to the correct definitions based on the words' contextual usage. Students should then have an understanding of the words when they meet them in the text.

After each reading assignment, students will go back and formulate answers for the study guide questions. Discussion of these questions serves as a **review** of the most important events and ideas presented in the reading assignments.

After students complete reading the work, a lesson is devoted to the **extra discussion questions/writing assignments**. These questions focus on interpretation, critical analysis and personal response, employing a variety of thinking skills and adding to the students' understanding of the novel.

There is a **vocabulary review** lesson which pulls together all of the fragmented vocabulary lists for the reading assignments and gives students a review of all of the words they have studied.

There are three **writing assignments** in this unit, each with the purpose of informing, persuading, or having students express personal opinions. The first assignment is to inform: students work together to create a report explaining what they will do for their presentation relating to the group presentation assignment. The second assignment is to persuade and to exercise creativity: students create a scenario in which they have discovered a treasure map and wish to go find the treasure. They are to write a composition stating what they would say to their parent(s) to persuade them to support the treasure hunt. The third assignment is to express personal opinions: students write a critical review of the book and the film version of *Treasure Island*.

There is a **nonfiction reading assignment**. Students are required to read a piece of nonfiction related in some way to *Treasure Island*  After reading their nonfiction pieces, students will fill out a worksheet on which they answer questions regarding facts, interpretation, criticism, and personal opinions. In this unit the nonfiction reading assignment is combined with a **group presentation project**. Students are divided into three groups: ships, pirates, and treasures. Each group is responsible for making a 15-20 minute creative presentation about its topic. The presentations are based on nonfiction reading--research-- students do relating to their topics.

The **review lesson** pulls together all of the aspects of the unit. The teacher is given four or five choices of activities or games to use which all serve the same basic function of reviewing all of the information presented in the unit.

The **unit test** comes in two formats: short answer or multiple choice. There are two regular short answer tests, one advanced short answer test, and two multiple choice tests. The tests cover a variety of levels and test-taking applications so you can choose the parts that are most appropriate for your students. Extra test materials could be used as make-up tests.

There are additional **support materials** included with this unit. The **extra activities** section includes suggestions for an in-class library, crossword and word search puzzles related to the novel, and extra vocabulary worksheets. There is a list of **bulletin board ideas** which gives the teacher suggestions for bulletin boards to go along with this unit. In addition, there is a list of **extra class activities** the teacher could choose from to enhance the unit or as a substitution for an exercise the teacher might feel is inappropriate for his/her class. **Answer keys** are located directly after the **reproducible student materials** throughout the unit. The student materials may be reproduced for use in the teacher's classroom without infringement of copyrights. No other portion of this unit may be reproduced without the written consent of Teacher's Pet Publications, Inc.

# UNIT OBJECTIVES - *Treasure Island*

1. Through reading Robert Louis Stevenson's *Treasure Island*, students will study the components of a tale of adventure set in an era long gone.

2. Students will demonstrate their understanding of the text on four levels: factual, interpretive, critical, and personal.

3. Students will investigate real pirates, treasures, and shipwrecks.

4. Students will be given the opportunity to practice reading aloud and silently to improve their skills in each area.

5. Students will answer questions to demonstrate their knowledge and understanding of the main events and characters in *Treasure Island* as they relate to the author's theme development.

6. Students will enrich their vocabularies and improve their understanding of the novel through the vocabulary lessons prepared for use in conjunction with the novel.

7. The writing assignments in this unit are geared to several purposes:
    a. To have students demonstrate their abilities to inform, to persuade, or to express their own personal ideas
        NOTE: Students will demonstrate ability to write effectively to <u>inform</u> by developing and organizing facts to convey information. Students will demonstrate the ability to write effectively to <u>persuade</u> by selecting and organizing relevant information, establishing an argumentative purpose, and by designing an appropriate strategy for an identified audience. Students will demonstrate the ability to write effectively to <u>express personal ideas</u> by selecting a form and its appropriate elements.
    b. To check the students' reading comprehension
    c. To make students think about the ideas presented by the novel
    d. To encourage logical thinking
    e. To provide an opportunity to practice good grammar and improve students' use of the English language.

8. Students will read aloud, report, and participate in large and small group discussions to improve their public speaking and personal interaction skills.

## READING ASSIGNMENT SHEET - *Treasure Island*

| Date Assigned | Reading Assignments | Completion Date |
|---|---|---|
| | Part I | |
| | Part II | |
| | Part III | |
| | Part IV | |
| | Part V | |
| | Part VI | |

## UNIT OUTLINE - *Treasure Island*

| 1<br><br>Introduction<br>PV I | 2<br><br>Read I | 3<br><br>Study ?s I<br>PVR II | 4<br><br>Study ?s II<br>PVR III | 5<br><br>Library |
|---|---|---|---|---|
| 6<br><br>Study ?s III<br>PVR IV<br>Group Work | 7<br><br>Study ?s IV<br>Group Work<br>PVR V | 8<br><br>Writing Assignment #1 | 9<br><br>Study ?s V<br>PVR VI | 10<br><br>Study ?s VI<br>Extra Questions |
| 11<br><br>Vocabulary | 12<br><br>Group Presentations | 13<br><br>Writing Assignment #2 | 14<br><br>Film | 15<br><br>Film |
| 16<br><br>Writing Assignment #3 | 17<br><br>Review | 18<br><br>Test | | |

Key: P = Preview Study Questions  V = Vocabulary Work  R = Read

# STUDY GUIDE QUESTIONS

# SHORT ANSWER STUDY GUIDE QUESTIONS - *Treasure Island*

## PART I
1. Identify Dr. Livesey, Admiral Benbow, Bill Bones, Black Dog, Jim, and Pew.
2. Why did Captain Bill Bones come to the Admiral Benbow?
3. What duty did Jim do for the captain?
4. Was the captain's presence at the inn good or bad for business? Why?
5. Who was the only man who stood up to Captain Bill Bones?
6. Why didn't Captain Bill Bones kill Black Dog?
7. What diagnosis did the doctor make after examining Captain Bones, and what remedy did he recommend?
8. For what reason did Pew come to see Captain Bill Bones?
9. Why did Jim and Mrs. Hawkins go to the neighboring hamlet after Captain Bones' death?
10. How did Jim and Mrs. Hawkins discover the map?
11. For what reason did Jim ride with Dogger to see Dr. Livesey?
12. After he had seen the contents of the oilcloth, what plans did the squire make?

## PART II
1. Name the ship and the cook John Trelawney found for the trip to Treasure Island.
2. Why didn't Jim think Long John Silver was a pirate when he first met him?
3. What were Captain Smollett's complaints to the squire?
4. Was Mr. Arrow a good officer? Why or why not?
5. What did Jim hear while he was in the apple barrel?

## PART III
1. Why did the captain give the men an afternoon ashore when they arrived at the island?
2. What was Jim's first "mad notion"?
3. What did Jim witness from his hiding place in the thicket?
4. Who was the "Man of the Island"? How did he get there?

## PART IV
1. Who narrates chapters 16 and 17? Why?
2. Why did Trelawney shoot one of the men who was with Hands?
3. Who was the first of the doctor's men to die?
4. What message was Jim to deliver to the squire or the doctor for Ben Gunn?
5. What did Jim's group decide would be their "best hope" for survival?
6. What truce offer did Long John Silver make to Captain Smollett, and what was Smollett's response?
7. What was the outcome of the pirates' attack on the stockade?

*Treasure Island* Short Answer Study Questions Page 2

## PART V
1. What was Jim's "second folly"?
2. How did Jim get out to the ship?
3. On the morning after Jim set the *Hispaniola* adrift, why did he board her?
4. What deal did Israel Hands make with Jim?
5. Why did Israel Hands send Jim to get him some wine?
6. How did Israel Hands die?
7. Who did Jim find upon his return to the blockhouse?

## PART VI
1. How did Silver get possession of the blockhouse?
2. What was Jim's deal with Silver?
3. Why did the council give Silver the black spot?
4. Why did the council decide to invalidate the black spot and keep Silver as captain?
5. What scared the treasure-hunting pirates?
6. What surprise did Silver and the pirates find at the treasure site?
7. Who saved Silver and Jim?
8. Who got the treasure?
9. What happened to Silver?
10. What happened to the others?

# ANSWER KEY: SHORT ANSWER STUDY GUIDE QUESTIONS - *Treasure Island*

## PART I

1. Identify Dr. Livesey, Admiral Benbow, Bill Bones, Black Dog, Jim, and Pew.
    **Dr. Livesey** tended to Mr. Hawkins during his illness. He was a magistrate and a member of the group that went to Treasure Island.
    **Admiral Benbow** was the name of the inn owned by Hawkins and visited by Bill Bones.
    **Black Dog** was the man who came to the inn looking for Bill. His identifying characteristic was that he was missing two fingers.
    **Jim Hawkins** is the boy narrator of the story.
    **Pew** was the blind buccaneer who delivered the black spot to Bill and was later trampled by a horse and killed.

2. Why did Captain Bill Bones come to the Admiral Benbow?
    He was apparently looking for a comfortable out-of-the-way place to stay where the other pirates couldn't find him and the treasure map.

3. What duty did Jim do for the captain?
    He kept a lookout for a man with one leg.

4. Was the captain's presence at the inn good or bad for business? Why?
    Mr. Hawkins thought it was bad because the captain would frighten people away, but Jim thought it might be good because people enjoyed the captain's stories--even if they were scared of him.

5. Who was the only man who stood up to Captain Bill Bones?
    Dr. Livesey did.

6. Why didn't Captain Bill Bones kill Black Dog?
    His sword hit the inn's wooden sign instead of Black Dog, and Black Dog ran away.

7. What diagnosis did the doctor make after examining Captain Bones, and what remedy did he recommend?
    He said that the captain had had a stroke. He took out some of the captain's blood, told him to stop overindulging in rum, and told him to rest at least for a week.

8. For what reason did Pew come to see Captain Bill Bones?
    He came to give him the "black spot," his death notice.

9. Why did Jim and Mrs. Hawkins go to the neighboring hamlet after Captain Bones' death?
    Since Mr. Hawkins died, they thought they might need help in case Pew and the other pirates would return.

10. How did Jim and Mrs. Hawkins discover the map?
    Mrs. Hawkins had Jim search through the captain's things looking for money and valuables which would settle his account with the inn. There wasn't enough money to square the account, so Jim took the oilskin packet to complete the payment.

11. For what reason did Jim ride with Dogger to see Dr. Livesey?
    Since Dr. Livesey was a magistrate, Jim thought the oilcloth would be safest in his keeping.

12. After he had seen the contents of the oilcloth, what plans did the squire make?
    He said that he, Dr. Livesey, Jim, Redruth, Joyce, and Hunter would sail for Treasure Island within a few weeks to search for the treasure.

## PART II
1. Name the ship and the cook John Trelawney found for the trip to Treasure Island.
    The ship was the *Hispaniola*, and the cook was Long John Silver.

2. Why didn't Jim think Long John Silver was a pirate when he first met him?
    Silver was a "clean and pleasant-tempered landlord," not at all like the buccaneers he had previously met.

3. What were Captain Smollett's complaints to the squire?
    He didn't like the cruise, the men, or his officer.

4. Was Mr. Arrow a good officer? Why or why not?
    No, he was not a good officer. He had "no command among the men" and he was often drunk.

5. What did Jim hear while he was in the apple barrel?
    He learned that John Silver and many of the crew members he recruited were part of Flint's old crew. They were pirates after the treasure and were likely to make trouble.

## PART III
1. Why did the captain give the men an afternoon ashore when they arrived at the island?
    The captain wanted to give John Silver the opportunity to talk to the men and get them in order to avoid mutiny as long as possible.

2. What was Jim's first "mad notion"?
    He stowed away on one of the boats going to shore that first afternoon.

3. What did Jim witness from his hiding place in the thicket?
    He saw John Silver kill Tom, a mate who would have been loyal to Captain Smollett.

4. Who was the "Man of the Island"? How did he get there?
    Ben Gunn was marooned there three years before. He had told his shipmates about the treasure, but after twelve days of unsuccessful searching, they were so angry with Ben (thinking he had led them on a wild goose chase) that they left him on the island.

## PART IV

1. Who narrates chapters 16 and 17? Why?
    The doctor narrates these chapters which give us information about important events in which Jim did not participate.

2. Why did Trelawney shoot one of the men who was with Hands?
    Five of Silver's men were preparing to use the long nine gun against the doctor's group. The doctor asked Trelawney (the best shot among them) to shoot Israel Hands, but Hands ducked and the shot hit another mate.

3. Who was the first of the doctor's men to die?
    Tom Redruth was shot and killed in the first day at the stockade.

4. What message was Jim to deliver to the squire or the doctor for Ben Gunn?
    Ben wanted to meet one of them to discuss a proposal. Jim was to be sure to tell them that Ben Gunn was a "precious sight" and that Ben had "reasons of his own."

5. What did Jim's group decide would be their "best hope" for survival?
    They would kill as many of the buccaneers as possible and use their supplies to survive.

6. What truce offer did Long John Silver make to Captain Smollett, and what was Smollett's response?
    Silver proposed that Smollett would hand over the treasure map and stop killing Silver's men. In exchange Silver would give his word of honor that Smollett's men would have safe passage to another port or he would send another ship to pick them up from the island. Captain Smollett's reply was that if Silver's men would come up one by one, he would place them in irons and take them to a fair trial in England. Otherwise, he'd "see [them] all to Davy Jones."

7. What was the outcome of the pirates' attack on the stockade?
    Five buccaneers were killed. Of Captain Smollett's men, Hunter was "stunned" (and later died), Joyce was dead, and the captain and the squire were wounded.

## PART V

1. What was Jim's "second folly"?
    He left two men guarding the stockade and went out to cut the *Hispaniola* adrift.

2. How did Jim get out to the ship?
    He took Ben Gunn's homemade boat.

3. On the morning after Jim set the *Hispaniola* adrift, why did he board her?
    It seemed as though no one was sailing her, and he hoped to return her to Captain Smollett.

4. What deal did Israel Hands make with Jim?
    Jim was to feed Hands and help mend his wounds, and Hands would help Jim sail the ship.

5. Why did Israel Hands send Jim to get him some wine?
>He wanted to be alone so he could get a weapon with which he could kill Jim.

6. How did Israel Hands die?
>When he threw his knife at Jim, pinning him by the shoulder to the mast, both of Jim's pistols went off, and Hands plunged into the water.

7. Who did Jim find upon his return to the blockhouse?
>He found Silver and his men.

## PART VI

1. How did Silver get possession of the blockhouse?
>Upon seeing that the ship was gone, Dr. Livesey went to Silver with a flag of truce. He turned over the stores, blockhouse, and firewood to Silver and his men.

2. What was Jim's deal with Silver?
>If Silver would spare his life, Jim would stand up for Silver in court and do all he could to save his life.

3. Why did the council give Silver the black spot?
>They thought he had bungled the cruise, let the enemy get away for nothing, protected the enemy at the marsh, and made an alliance with Jim.

4. Why did the council decide to invalidate the black spot and keep Silver as captain?
>Silver showed them Flint's treasure map.

5. What scared the treasure-hunting pirates?
>First they found a skeleton and then they heard the chorus of "Fifteen men . . ." and a voice which repeated Flint's last words. They thought that Flint's ghost was on the island.

6. What surprise did Silver and the pirates find at the treasure site?
>The treasure had already been found and removed.

7. Who saved Silver and Jim?
>The doctor, Gray, and Ben Gunn shot three of the mates who were about to mutiny. The other three ran away.

8. Who got the treasure?
>Ben Gunn had found it and stored it away two months before the *Hispaniola* had arrived.

9. What happened to Silver?
>He escaped from the ship at the first port they found in Spanish America, taking a sack of treasure with him.

10. What happened to the others?
>The three remaining mutineers were left with provisions on the island. Captain Smollett's men all got their shares of the treasure and did with it as they pleased after they returned safely to Bristol.

# MULTIPLE CHOICE STUDY GUIDE/QUIZ QUESTIONS - *Treasure Island*

Part I
1-4 Match each character with the correct description:

1. Dr. Livesey
2. Jim
3. Capt. Bill Bones
4. Black Dog

A. He was missing two fingers
B. He was a magistrate and went to Treasure Island
C. He was given the Black Spot
D. He was the narrator of the story

5. Identify Admiral Benbow.
   a. Admiral Benbow was a retired merchant who was visiting England.
   b. Admiral Benbow was a writer who wanted a quiet place to work for a few weeks.
   c. Admiral Benbow was the name of a famous pirate ship that had terrorized the seas for many years.
   d. Admiral Benbow was the name of the inn owned by Jim's family.

6. True or False: Pew was the blind buccaneer who delivered the Black Spot.
   a. True
   b. False

7. Why did Captain Bill Bones come to the inn?
   a. He was recovering from a bad case of scurvy and had orders from his doctor to rest.
   b. He was looking for a comfortable out-of-the-way place to stay where the other pirates couldn't find him and the treasure map.
   c. He wanted to assemble a crew to go and find the treasure.
   d. He wanted to give up his old life and start over again. He was hoping to buy the inn and become a respectable innkeeper.

8. What duty did Jim do for the captain?
   a. He brought the captain the newspaper every day.
   b. He took messages into town and brought answers back to the inn.
   c. He played checkers with the captain every day.
   d. He kept a lookout for a man with one leg.

9. Which of the following statements is true concerning the captain's presence at the inn?
   a. Mr. Hawkins and Jim both thought it was a bad idea to have him there because he would frighten other people away.
   b. Jim thought it was a bad idea because the captain was noisy and rude, but Mr. Hawkins wanted the money.
   c. Mr. Hawkins thought it was bad because the captain would frighten people away, but Jim thought it might be good because people enjoyed the captain's stories, even if they were scared of him.
   d. Both of them thought it was good for business to have such a character around, but Jim's mother was afraid of him and said he could not stay.

*Treasure Island* Multiple Choice Study/Quiz Questions Page 2

10. Who was the only man who stood up to Captain Bill Bones?
    a. Dr. Livesey
    b. Jim
    c. Black Dog
    d. Pew

11. Why didn't Captain Bill Bones kill Black Dog?
    a. Jim's mother screamed and startled him, and he dropped his sword.
    b. He thought Black Dog might be useful to him at a later time.
    c. Two other patrons came into the inn just as he was about to kill Black Dog.
    d. His sword hit the inn's wooden sign instead of Black Dog, and Black Dog ran away.

12. True or False: The doctor said that the captain had a bad case of gout. He prescribed fresh air and exercise as the remedy.
    a. True
    b. False

13. For what reason did Pew come to see Captain Bill Bones?
    a. To buy the treasure map
    b. To blackmail him
    c. To give him the Black Spot, his death notice
    d. To kill him

14. Where did Jim and Mrs. Hawkins go after Captain Bones' death?
    a. They went to the neighboring hamlet to get help.
    b. They barricaded themselves in the inn.
    c. They went to the police station.
    d. They went to the doctor's office.

15. How did Jim and Mrs. Hawkins discover the map?
    a. It was lying out on the captain's bed when they went into his room.
    b. It fell out of his pocket when they moved the body.
    c. He gave it to them just before he died.
    d. They were searching through his things looking for money. When they didn't find enough, Jim took the oilskin pack.

16. For what reason did Jim ride with Dogger to see Doctor Livesey?
    a. He wanted the doctor to perform an autopsy.
    b. Since Doctor Livesey was a magistrate, Jim thought the oilcloth would be safest in his keeping.
    c. Mrs. Hawkins had taken ill after the recent events. Jim was going to get medicine.
    d. He could not read and he was going to ask Doctor Livesey to read the contents of the oilskin to him.

*Treasure Island* Multiple Choice Study/Quiz Questions Page 3

17. After he had seen the contents of the oilcloth, what plans did the squire make?
    a. He said that he, Doctor Livesey, Jim, Redruth, Joyce, and Hunter would sail for Treasure Island within a few weeks to search for the treasure.
    b. He planned to kill Jim to get sole possession of the map.
    c. He was afraid to keep the map himself, and he made arrangements to give it to the pastor to keep.
    d. He wanted to buy the map from Jim so that he could get the treasure for himself.

*Treasure Island* Multiple Choice Study/Quiz Questions Page 4

Part II

18. Name the ship and the cook John Trelawney found for the trip to Treasure Island.
    a. *The Silver Bird* was the ship, and the cook was Fierce Tom Johnson.
    b. The ship was *The Aquiola*, and the cook was Peg Leg Harwig.
    c. The ship was the *Hispaniola*, and the cook was Long John Silver.
    d. *The Panatera* was the ship, and the cook was Grey Beard Derek.

19. What did Jim think of the cook?
    a. He was instantly suspicious and thought he looked like a pirate.
    b. He thought the cook looked clean and pleasant-tempered.
    c. The cook reminded him of his father, though he was not as well skilled in social graces as his father.
    d. Jim was repulsed by the cook.

20. Captain Smollett had several complaints that he voiced to the squire. Which of the following was ***not*** one of his complaints?
    a. He didn't like the food.
    b. He didn't like the cruise.
    c. He didn't like the men.
    d. He didn't like his officer.

21. Was Mr. Arrow a good officer?
    a. Yes. He had the men's respect and was always alert.
    b. No. He had no command among the men and was frequently drunk.

22. True or False: While Jim was in the apple barrel, he learned that John Silver and many of the crew members were part of Flint's old crew.
    a. True
    b. False

*Treasure Island* Multiple Choice Study/Quiz Questions Page 5

Part III

23. Why did the captain give the men an afternoon ashore when they arrived at the island?
    a. He needed time to rest himself because he had been sick on the voyage.
    b. He needed time to think about what to do.
    c. He wanted to give Long John Silver the opportunity to talk to the men and get them in order to avoid mutiny as long as possible.
    d. He was planning to steal the ship and sail back home without them.

24. What was Jim's first "mad notion"?
    a. He stole a gun and hid it under his shirt.
    b. He stowed away on one of the boats going ashore that first afternoon.
    c. He tried to poison the food.
    d. He put a message asking for help in a bottle and threw it overboard.

25. What did Jim witness from his hiding place in the thicket?
    a. He saw Long John Silver kill Tom, a mate who would have been loyal to Captain Smollett.
    b. He saw Captain Smollett throwing supplies overboard.
    c. He saw two of the crewmen putting a hole in the bottom of the rowboat.
    d. He saw Mr. Arrow giving a piece of paper and a handful of coins to Long John Silver.

26. True or False: Ben Gunn had been marooned on the island because his shipmates were angry when they didn't find the treasure he said was there.
    a. True
    b. False

*Treasure Island* Multiple Choice Study/Quiz Questions Page 6

Part IV

27. True or False: Ben Gunn is the narrator of chapters 16 and 17.
    a. True
    b. False

28. Why did Trelawney shoot one of the men who was with Hands?
    a. He had worked with the man before and did not like him.
    b. He was nervous and the gun went off before he intended for it to.
    c. He was supposed to shoot Hands, but he ducked and the shot hit another mate.
    d. The doctor thought that if they shot enough of the men, Hands would surrender.

29. Who was the first of the doctor's men to die?
    a. David Flint
    b. John Hunter
    c. Richard Joyce
    d. Tom Redruth

30. True or False: The following statement is the message Ben Gunn told Jim to deliver to the squire or the doctor: "And when Ben Gunn is wanted, you know where to find him . . . And him that comes is to have a white thing in his hand: and he is to come alone . . . Ben Gunn has reasons of his own."
    a. True
    b. False

31. What did Jim's group decide would be their best hope for survival?
    a. They would go back to the ship and try to sail away.
    b. They would burn down all of the vegetation on the island to expose the buccaneers.
    c. They would kill as many of the buccaneers as possible and use their supplies to survive.
    d. They would try to make a deal with the buccaneers to split all of the profits when they found the treasure.

32. True or False: Silver proposed that Smollett would hand over the treasure map and stop killing Silver's men. In return, Silver would give Smollett's men safe passage to another port.
    a. True
    b. False

33. True of False: Smollett replied that if Silver's men would come up one-by-one, he would place them in irons and take them to a fair trial in England. Otherwise, he'd "see them all to Davy Jones."
    a. True
    b. False

*Treasure Island* Multiple Choice Study/Quiz Questions Page 7

34. What was the outcome of the pirates' attack on the stockade?
    a. Two buccaneers were killed, Captain Smollett was wounded, and Joyce was wounded.
    b. Long John Silver was wounded, three of his men were killed, Hunter and Joyce were killed, and the squire was wounded.
    c. Only one buccaneer was killed, but all of Smollett's men were either killed or wounded.
    d. Five buccaneers were killed, Captain Smollett and the squire were wounded, and Hunter and Joyce died.

*Treasure Island* Multiple Choice Study/Quiz Questions Page 8

Part V

35. Who left two men guarding the stockade while he went to cut the *Hispanola*?
    a. Captain Smollett
    b. Mr. Arrow
    c. Jim
    d. The squire

36. On this morning after the *Hispanola* was set adrift, Jim boarded her. Why did he do this?
    a. He wanted to get more food supplies.
    b. He was looking for extra weapons and gunpowder.
    c. It seemed as though no one was sailing her, and he hoped to return her to Captain Smollett.
    d. He had decided to set her afire so that the buccaneers would not be able to use her at all.

37. True of False: Israel Hands told Jim that if Jim would let him free, Israel would share half of the treasure with him.
    a. True
    b. False

38. Why did Israel Hands send Jim to get him some wine?
    a. He wanted to be alone so he could get a weapon with which he could kill Jim.
    b. He was in pain and he wanted to get drunk and forget about it.
    c. He wanted to get Jim drunk so that he could make Jim disclose his group's plans.
    d. He was planning to lock Jim up in the hold when he went down for wine.

39. How did Israel Hands die?
    a. Jim had poisoned the wine. Israel drank it and died almost immediately.
    b. He lunged at Jim, who ducked. The momentum carried Israel overboard.
    c. When he threw his knife at Jim, pinning him by the shoulder to the mast, both of Jim's pistols went off, and Hands plunged into the water.
    d. Jim had been able to sneak around behind Hands. He told Hands to put down the knife and turn around. When Hands refused, Jim shot him.

40. Who did Jim find upon his return to the blockhouse?
    a. He found the squire and the doctor.
    b. He found Ben Gunn.
    c. No one. He found that the blockhouse was deserted.
    d. He found Silver and his men.

*Treasure Island* Multiple Choice Study/Quiz Questions Page 9

Part VI

41. True of False: Silver had offered Dr. Livesey half of the treasure if he would join forces with him. Dr. Livesey agreed.
    a. True
    b. False

42. What was Jim's deal with Silver?
    a. Jim only wanted safe passage home. He promised he would never speak of the search for the treasure.
    b. Jim wanted to join the buccaneers. He thought that if he acted like one of Silver's men, he would have more a chance of escaping at a later time.
    c. If Silver would spare his life, Jim would stand up for Silver in court and do all he could to save his life.
    d. Jim asked to be left on the island and for Silver to send a rescue ship after him.

43. What did the council do?
    a. They gave Silver half the treasure for a job well done.
    b. They gave Silver the "Black Spot" for bungling the job and letting the enemy get away.
    c. They gave Silver a promotion and a medal for his bravery in an adverse situation.
    d. They stripped Silver of his rank, flogged him, and put him in jail for one year.

44. Did the council follow through with their original decision?
    a. Yes
    b. No

45. Which of the following was not one of the things that scared the treasure-hunting pirates?
    a. They found a skeleton.
    b. They heard a chorus of "Fifteen men . . .."
    c. They heard each of their names called by a mysterious, ghostly voice.
    d. They heard a voice repeat Flint's last words.

46. What surprise did Silver and the pirates find at the treasure site?
    a. The treasure had already been found and removed.
    b. There was twice as much treasure as they had expected.
    c. There was a flag with a skull and crossbones with a written warning.
    d. The treasure was booby-trapped.

47. What happened to the men?
    a. The doctor and Gray were killed along with two of the pirates.
    b. Ben Gunn was wounded, but all six of the pirates were killed.
    c. Gray and Ben Gunn were killed, Silver was wounded, and four of the six pirates were killed.
    d. The doctor, Gray, and Ben Gunn shot three of the mates who were about to mutiny. The other three got away.

*Treasure Island* Multiple Choice Study/Quiz Questions Page 10

48. Who got the treasure?
    a. Silver had found it and hidden it.
    b. Jim had taken it aboard the *Hispanola*.
    c. Ben Gunn had found it and stored it away before the *Hispanola* had arrived.
    d. The doctor had managed to get it and hide it on the other side of the island.

49. What happened to Silver?
    a. He returned to Bristol, was tried, and spent the rest of his life in prison.
    b. He escaped from the ship at the first port they found in Spanish America, taking a sack of treasure with him.
    c. He killed himself, saying it was preferable to a life in prison.
    d. He escaped when they reached Bristol, saying he would spend the rest of his life hunting them down and seeking revenge.

50. What happened to the remaining mutineers?
    a. They were left with provisions on the island.
    b. They were tried and killed by Captain Smollett and the others before they all left the island.
    c. Long John Silver killed them because they had failed him and to keep them from testifying against him.
    d. They tried to swim after the *Hispanola* as it sailed away. Two were eaten by sharks and the third returned to the island, stranded.

51. True or False: Captain Smollett kept all of the treasure and only paid the crew members a small part of their rightful share.
    a. True
    b. False

## ANSWER KEY - MULTIPLE CHOICE STUDY/QUIZ QUESTIONS
*Treasure Island*

| Part I | Part II | Part III | Part IV | Part V | Part VI |
|---|---|---|---|---|---|
| 1. b | 18. c | 23. c | 27. b | 35. c | 41. b |
| 2. d | 19. b | 24. b | 28. c | 36. c | 42. c |
| 3. c | 20. a | 25. a | 29. d | 37. b | 43. b |
| 4. a | 21. b | 26. a | 30. a | 38. a | 44. b |
| 5. d | 22. a | | 31. c | 39. c | 45. c |
| 6. a | | | 32. a | 40. d | 46. a |
| 7. b | | | 33. b | | 47. d |
| 8. d | | | 34. d | | 48. c |
| 9. c | | | | | 49. b |
| 10. a | | | | | 50. a |
| 11. d | | | | | 51. b |
| 12. b | | | | | |
| 13. c | | | | | |
| 14. a | | | | | |
| 15. d | | | | | |
| 16. b | | | | | |
| 17. a | | | | | |

# PREREADING VOCABULARY WORKSHEETS

# VOCABULARY - *Treasure Island*

Part I: Using Prior Knowledge and Contextual Clues

Below are the sentences in which the vocabulary words appear in the text. Read the sentence. Use any clues you can find in the sentence combined with your prior knowledge, and write what you think the underlined words mean on the lines provided.

1. . . . and go back to the time when my father kept the "Admiral Benbow" inn, and the brown old seaman, with the <u>sabre</u> cut, first took up his lodging under our roof.

   _____

2. . . . a tall, strong, heavy, nut-brown man; his <u>tarry</u> pigtail falling over the shoulders of his soiled blue coat; . . .

   _____

3. . . . and then breaking out in that old sea-song that he sang so often afterwards: *"Fifteen men on the dead man's chest--Yo-ho-ho, and a bottle of rum!"* in the high, old tottering voice that seemed to have been tuned and broken at the <u>capstan</u> bars.

   _____

4. This, when it was brought to him, he drank slowly, like a <u>connoisseur</u> lingering on the taste, and still looking about him at the cliffs and up at our signboard.

   _____

5. How that <u>personage</u> haunted my dreams, I need scarcely tell you.

   _____

6. "Were you addressing me, sir?" says the doctor; and when the <u>ruffian</u> had told him, with another oath, that this was so, "I have only one thing to say to you, sir," replies the doctor, "that if you keep on drinking rum, the world will soon be quit of a very dirty scoundrel!"

   _____

7. He was a pale, <u>tallowy</u> creature, wanting two fingers of the left hand; and, though he wore a cutlass, he did not look much like a fighter.

   _____

8. The captain had been struck dead by thundering <u>apoplexy</u>.

   _____

Vocabulary - *Treasure Island* Part I Continued

9. Overcoming a strong repugnance, I tore open his shirt at the neck, and there, sure enough, hanging to a bit of tarry string, which I cut with his own gully, we found the key.

_____

10. "I'll have my dues, and not a farthing over.

_____


Part II:  Determining the Meaning
   Match the vocabulary words to their dictionary definitions.  If there are words for which you cannot figure out the definition by contextual clues and by process of elimination, look them up in a dictionary.

____ 1. sabre  
____ 2. tarry  
____ 3. capstan  
____ 4. connoisseur  
____ 5. personage  
____ 6. ruffian  
____ 7. tallowy  
____ 8. apoplexy  
____ 9. repugnance  
____ 10. farthing  

A. physical form or bearing;  a person of distinction  
B. like tar;  to linger or delay  
C. one competent to act as a critical judge of an art or in a matter of taste.  
D. a cavalry sword with a somewhat curved blade for cutting and thrusting  
E. a small British bronze coin worth one fourth of a penny;  a very small quantity or value  
F. aversion;  loathing  
G. a vertical-cleated drum or cylinder revolving on a spindle used for raising weights by traction upon a rope or cable passing around the drum  
H. a cruel, brutal person  
I. pertaining to the fat of beef or mutton which has been extracted by melting  
J. a stroke caused by a rupture or obstruction of an artery of the brain

Vocabulary - *Treasure Island* Part II

Part I: Using Prior Knowledge and Contextual Clues
　　Below are the sentences in which the vocabulary words appear in the text. Read the sentence. Use any clues you can find in the sentence combined with your prior knowledge, and write what you think the underlined words mean on the lines provided.

1. And I was going to sea myself; to sea in a schooner, with a piping boatswain and pig-tailed singing seamen; to sea, bound for an unknown island, and to seek for buried treasures!

_____

2. "Has Mr. Trelawney not told you of the buccaneers? He was one of them."

_____

3. "Now, Barbecue, tip us a stave," cried one voice.

_____

4. And the coxwain, Israel Hands, was a careful, wily, old, experienced seaman. . . . . . . .

_____

5. Double grog was going on the least excuse; there was duff on odd days, as for instance, if the squire heard it was any man's birthday; and always a barrel of apples standing broached in the waist, for anyone to help himself that had a fancy.

_____

6. "But," asked Dick, "when we do lay athwart, what are we to do with 'em, anyhow?"

_____

7. I was surprised at the coolness with which John avowed his knowledge of the island;..........

_____

8. "I never heard of a crew that meant to mutiny but what showed signs before, for any man that had an eye in his head to see the mischief and take steps according."

_____

35

Vocabulary - *Treasure Island* Part II Continued

Part II: Determining the Meaning   Match the vocabulary words to their dictionary definitions. If there are words for which you cannot figure out the definition by contextual clues and by process of elimination, look them up in a dictionary.

___ 11. boatswain
___ 12. buccaneers
___ 13. stave
___ 14. coxwain
___ 15. grog
___ 16. athwart
___ 17. avowed
___ 18. mutiny

A. the steersman of a ship's boat
B. declared openly; acknowledged; admitted
C. any intoxicating liquor
D. a warrant officer or superior seaman on a ship in charge of rigging, anchors, cables, etc.
E. insubordination; refusal to obey, especially military or naval authority
F. pirates, especially of the 17th and 18th centuries
G. in opposition to; across the length, direction or course of
H. a stick or cudgel; narrow strips to form the sides of a barrel; to break a hole in; to ward off

Vocabulary - *Treasure Island* Part III

Part I: Using Prior Knowledge and Contextual Clues

Below are the sentences in which the vocabulary words appear in the text. Read the sentence. Use any clues you can find in the sentence combined with your prior knowledge, and write what you think the underlined words mean on the lines provided.

1. "There's a strong scour with the ebb," he said, "and this here passage has been dug out, in a manner of speaking, with a spade."

   _____

2. Well, if I speak back, pikes will be going in two shakes; if I don't, Silver will see there's something under that, and the game's up.

   _____

3. . . . I had now come out upon the skirts of an open piece of undulating, sandy country, about a mile long, dotted with a few pines, and a great number of contorted trees. . .

   _____

4. This put me in a great fear, and I crawled under cover of the nearest live-oak, and squatted there, hearkening as silent as a mouse.

   _____

5. And now I began to feel that I was neglecting my business; that since I had been so foolhardy as to come ashore with these desperadoes, the least I could do was to overhear them at their councils; and that my plain and obvious duty was to draw as close as I could manage, under the favorable ambush of the crouching trees.

   _____

6. With a cry, John seized the branch of a tree, whipped the crutch out of his armpit, and sent that uncouth missile hurtling through the air.

   _____

7. I was now, it seemed, cut off upon both sides; behind me the murderers, before me this lurking nondescript.

   _____

Vocabulary - *Treasure Island* Part III Continued

8. "Three years!" I cried. "Were you shipwrecked?" "Nay, mate," said he, "---marooned."

_____

9. I now felt sure that the poor fellow had gone crazy in his solitude, and I suppose I must have shown the feeling in my face. . . . . . .

_____

10. Billy Bones was the mate; Long John, he was quartermaster; and they asked him where the treasure was.

_____

11. The cannon-shot was followed, after a considerable interval, by a volley of small arms.

_____

Part II: Determining the Meaning
Match the vocabulary words to their dictionary definitions. If there are words for which you cannot figure out the definition by contextual clues and by process of elimination, look them up in a dictionary.

|   |   |
|---|---|
| ___ 19. scour | A. to listen; to give heed to |
| ___ 20. pikes | B. not easily described; of no particular class or kind |
| ___ 21. undulating | C. simultaneous discharge of arrows, bullets or the like |
| ___ 22. hearkening | D. to make clean and bright by friction; to clear away; diarrhea in cattle |
| ___ 23. desperadoes | E. moving up and down or backward and forward; undulating |
| ___ 24. uncouth | F. an officer whose duty is to provide quarters, clothing, etc. for troops |
| ___ 25. nondescript | G. foot soldiers' weapons consisting of long wooden shafts with steel points |
| ___ 26. marooned | H. desperate criminals; law-breakers |
| ___ 27. solitude | I. unrefined; boorish; strange |
| ___ 28. quartermaster | J. state of being alone; seclusion |
| ___ 29. volley | K. to place or leave in hopeless isolation |

Vocabulary - *Treasure Island* Part IV

Part I: Using Prior Knowledge and Contextual Clues

Below are the sentences in which the vocabulary words appear in the text. Read the sentence. Use any clues you can find in the sentence combined with your prior knowledge, and write what you think the underlined words mean on the lines provided.

1. Well, on the knoll, and enclosing the spring, they had clapped a stout log-house, fit to hold two score people on a pinch, and loop-holed for <u>musketry</u> on every side.

   _____

2. Hunter brought the boat round under the sternport, and Joyce and I set to work loading her with powder tins, muskets, bags of biscuits, kegs of pork, a cask of <u>cognac</u>, and my invaluable medicine chest.

   _____

3. "If I <u>durst</u>," said the captain, "I'd stop and pick off another man."

   _____

4. Poor old fellow, he had not uttered one word of surprise, complaint, fear, or even <u>acquiescence</u>, from the very beginning of our troubles till now when we had laid him down in the log-house to die.

   _____

5. "Dr. Livesey," he said, "in how many weeks do you and squire expect the <u>consort</u>?"

   _____

6. We had no <u>ricochet</u> to fear; and though one popped in through the roof of the log-house and out again through the floor, we soon got used to that sort of horse-play, and minded it no more than cricket.

   _____

7. And, at that, up I jumped, and, rubbing my eyes, ran to a <u>loophole</u> in the wall.

   _____

Vocabulary - *Treasure Island* Part IV Continued

8. As for me, I began to have an inkling.

___

9. "Hang them!" said the captain. "This is as dull as the doldrums, Gray, whistle for a wind."

___

Part II: Determining the Meaning
   Match the vocabulary words to their dictionary definitions. If there are words for which you cannot figure out the definition by contextual clues and by process of elimination, look them up in a dictionary.

___ 30. musketry
___ 31. cognac
___ 32. durst
___ 33. acquiescence
___ 34. consort
___ 35. ricochet
___ 36. loophole
___ 37. inkling
___ 38. doldrums

A. a ship keeping company with another
B. act of complying passively without implying agreement
C. muskets; firearms carried by infantry
D. part of the ocean near the equator abounding in calms, squalls and baffling winds
E. dared; not afraid; to venture
F. a hint; a slight knowledge or vague notion
G. a superior French brandy from wine near Cognac; loosely, any French brandy
H. to skip with a glancing rebound or series of rebounds
I. a small opening through which small arms may be discharged

Vocabulary - *Treasure Island* Part V

Part I: Using Prior Knowledge and Contextual Clues
   Below are the sentences in which the vocabulary words appear in the text. Read the sentence. Use any clues you can find in the sentence combined with your prior knowledge, and write what you think the underlined words mean on the lines provided.

1. These biscuits, should anything befall me, would keep me, at least, from starving till far on in the next day.

   _____

2. This was my second folly, far worse than the first, as I left but two sound men to guard the house; but like the first, it was a help towards saving all of us.

   _____

3. Soon after the jolly-boat shoved off and pulled for shore, and the man with the red cap and his comrade went below by the cabin companion.

   _____

4. I had not then seen a coracle, such as the ancient Britons made, but I have seen one since, and I can give you no fairer idea of Ben Gunn's boat than by saying it was like the first and the worst coracle ever made by man.

   _____

5. At last the breeze came; the schooner sidled and drew nearer in the dark; I felt the hawser slacken once more, and with a good tough effort cut the last fibers through.

   _____

6. So I must have lain for hours, continually beaten to and fro upon the billows, and now and again wetted with flying sprays, and never ceasing to expect death at the next plunge.

   _____

Vocabulary - *Treasure Island* Part V Continued

7. Among the fallen rocks the breakers spouted and bellowed; loud <u>reverberations</u>, heavy sprays flying and falling, succeeded one another from second to second; and I saw myself, if I ventured nearer, dashed to death upon the rough shore, or spending my strength in vain to scale the beetling crags.

_____

8. . . . Israel Hands propped against the <u>bulwarks</u> his chin on his chest, his hands lying open before him on the deck, his face as white, under its tan, as a tallow candle.

_____

9. The excitement of these last maneuvers had somewhat interfered with the watch I had kept <u>hitherto</u>, sharply enough, upon the coxwain.

_____

10. I stole round by the eastern end, keeping close in shadow, and at a convenient place, where the darkness was thickest, crossed the <u>palisade</u>.

_____

Part II: Determining the Meaning
    Match the vocabulary words to their dictionary definitions. If there are words for which you cannot figure out the definition by contextual clues and by process of elimination, look them up in a dictionary.

        ___ 39. befall           A. until now
        ___ 40. folly            B. a boat made by covering a wicker frame with hide or cloth
        ___ 41. comrade          C. a fence of pales or stakes for defense; a line of bold cliffs
        ___ 42. coracle          D. to happen to
        ___ 43. sidled           E. echoes of sound
        ___ 44. billows          F. a mate; companion; associate
        ___ 45. reverberations   G. a foolish act or idea
        ___ 46. bulwarks         H. great waves or surges of water
        ___ 47. hitherto         I. moved sidewise
        ___ 48. palisade         J. the side of a ship above the upper deck; any strong safeguard

Vocabulary - *Treasure Island* Part VI

Part I: Using Prior Knowledge and Contextual Clues
    Below are the sentences in which the vocabulary words appear in the text. Read the sentence. Use any clues you can find in the sentence combined with your prior knowledge, and write what you think the underlined words mean on the lines provided.

1. But one thing I'll say, and no more; if you spare me, bygones are bygones, and when you fellows are in court for piracy, I'll save you all I can.

___

2. He drew some cognac from the cask into a tin cannikin.

___

3. . . . yet my heart was sore for him, wicked as he was, to think on the dark perils that environed, and the shameful gibbet that awaited him.

___

4. Although I was glad to hear the sound, yet my gladness was not without admixture.

___

5. . . . .Silver, if we both get alive out of this wolf-trap, I'll do my best to save you, short of perjury."

___

6. The *cache* had been found and rifled; the seven hundred thousand pounds were gone!

___

7. Merry tumbled head foremost into the excavation; the man with the bandage spun round like a teetotum, and fell all his length upon his side, where he lay dead, but still twitching; and the other three turned and ran for it with all their might.

___

Vocabulary - *Treasure Island* Part VI Continued

8. And there was Silver, sitting back almost out of the firelight, but eating heartily, prompt to spring forward when anything was wanted, even joining quietly in our laughter--the same bland, polite, <u>obsequious</u> seaman of the voyage out.

_____

9. Oxen and <u>wain-ropes</u> would not bring me back again to that accursed island; and the worst dreams that ever I have are when I hear the surf booming about its coasts, or start upright in bed, with the sharp voice of Captain Flint still ringing in my ears: "Pieces of eight! pieces of eight!"

_____

Part II: Determining the Meaning

Match the vocabulary words to their dictionary definitions. If there are words for which you cannot figure out the definition by contextual clues and by process of elimination, look them up in a dictionary.

| | | | |
|---|---|---|---|
| ___ 49. | bygones | A. | fawning; obedient; compliant |
| ___ 50. | cannikin | B. | false swearing; voluntary violation of an oath |
| ___ 51. | gibbet | C. | a cart rope; a trace or part of a harness |
| ___ 52. | admixture | D. | past; gone by |
| ___ 53. | perjury | E. | a child's toy somewhat like a top |
| ___ 54. | cache | F. | that which is added to anything by mixing |
| ___ 55. | teetotum | G. | a small can or drinking vessel |
| ___ 56. | obsequious | H. | a hole in the ground used for a hiding place for provisions, etc. |
| ___ 57. | wain-ropes | I. | a kind of gallows on which malefactors were hung in chains and allowed to remain there as a warning |

# ANSWER KEY: VOCABULARY - *Treasure Island*

| Part I | Part II | Part III | Part IV | Part V | Part VI |
|---|---|---|---|---|---|
| 1. D | 11. D | 19. D | 30. C | 39. D | 49. D |
| 2. B | 12. F | 20. G | 31. G | 40. G | 50. G |
| 3. G | 13. H | 21. E | 32. E | 41. F | 51. I |
| 4. C | 14. A | 22. A | 33. B | 42. B | 52. F |
| 5. A | 15. C | 23. H | 34. A | 43. I | 53. B |
| 6. H | 16. G | 24. I | 35. H | 44. H | 54. H |
| 7. I | 17. B | 25. B | 36. I | 45. E | 55. E |
| 8. J | 18. E | 26. K | 37. F | 46. J | 56. A |
| 9. F | | 27. J | 38. D | 47. A | 57. C |
| 10. E | | 28. F | | 48. C | |
| | | 29. C | | | |

# DAILY LESSONS

## LESSON ONE

Objectives
1. To introduce the *Treasure Island* unit.
2. To distribute books and other related materials

NOTE: Prior to this lesson, tell students to bring in pictures of something they treasure. They can be snapshots of the actual things or cut-out or drawn pictures--anything that can be stapled to the bulletin board. In addition, prior to this lesson you need to have prepared your bulletin board with background paper, a title (even something simple like TREASURES), an outline of an open treasure chest (which students will "fill up" with their pictures), and some cut-out or drawn scenery like palm trees to make the board look like a tropical island.

Activity #1
Tell students to get out their pictures (or whatever represents their treasures). Have students explain how or why the pictures (or items) represent their treasures. As each student explains his/her item, he/she should post it on the bulletin board in the treasure chest. If the treasure chest fills up, the treasures can spill over out of the chest onto the "ground."

TRANSITION: Explain that the class will be reading about treasures and pirates in the story they are about to read, *Treasure Island*.

Activity #2
Distribute the materials students will use in this unit. Explain in detail how students are to use these materials.

Study Guides  Students should read the study guide questions for each reading assignment prior to beginning the reading assignment to get a feeling for what events and ideas are important in the section they are about to read. After reading the section, students will (as a class or individually) answer the questions to review the important events and ideas from that section of the book. Students should keep the study guides as study materials for the unit test.

Vocabulary  Prior to reading a reading assignment, students will do vocabulary work related to the section of the book they are about to read. Following the completion of the reading of the book, there will be a vocabulary review of all the words used in the vocabulary assignments. Students should keep their vocabulary work as study materials for the unit test.

Reading Assignment Sheet  You need to fill in the reading assignment sheet to let students know by when their reading has to be completed. You can either write the assignment sheet up on a side blackboard or bulletin board and leave it there for students to see each day, or you can "ditto" copies for each student to have. In either case, you should advise students to become very familiar with the reading assignments so they know what is expected of them.

Extra Activities Center   The resource sections of this unit contain suggestions for an extra library of related books and articles in your classroom as well as crossword and word search puzzles.  Make an extra activities center in your room where you will keep these materials for students to use. (Bring the books and articles in from the library and keep several copies of the puzzles on hand.) Explain to students that these materials are available for students to use when they finish reading assignments or other class work early.

Nonfiction Assignment Sheet   Explain to students that they each are to read at least one non-fiction piece at some time during the unit. Students will fill out a nonfiction assignment sheet after completing the reading to help you evaluate their reading experiences and to help the students think about and evaluate their own reading experiences.

Books   Each school has its own rules and regulations regarding student use of school books. Advise students of the procedures that are normal for your school.

Activity #3
Preview the study questions and have students do the vocabulary work for Part I of *Treasure Island*. If students do not finish this assignment during this class period, they should complete it prior to the next class meeting.

# NONFICTION ASSIGNMENT SHEET
(To be completed after reading the required nonfiction article)

Name _____ Date _____

Title of Nonfiction Read _____

Written By _____ Publication Date _____

I. Factual Summary: Write a short summary of the piece you read.



II. Vocabulary
   1. With which vocabulary words in the piece did you encounter some degree of difficulty?


   2. How did you resolve your lack of understanding with these words?

III. Interpretation: What was the main point the author wanted you to get from reading his work?



IV. Criticism
   1. With which points of the piece did you agree or find easy to accept? Why?


   2. With which points of the piece did you disagree or find difficult to believe? Why?

V. Personal Response: What do you think about this piece? OR How does this piece influence your ideas?

## LESSON TWO

Objectives
    1. To read Part I
    3. To give students practice reading orally
    4. To evaluate students' oral reading

Activity #1
    Have students read Part I of *Treasure Island* out loud in class. You probably know the best way to get readers with your class; pick students at random, ask for volunteers, or use whatever method works best for your group. If you have not yet completed an oral reading evaluation for your students this marking period, this would be a good opportunity to do so. A form is included with this unit for your convenience.
    If students do not complete reading Part I in class, they should do so prior to your next class meeting.

## LESSON THREE

Objectives
    1. To review the main ideas and events from Part I
    2. To do the prereading work for Part II
    3. To read Part II
    4. To complete the oral reading evaluations

Activity #1
    Give students a few minutes to formulate answers for the study guide questions for Part I and then discuss the answers to the questions in detail. Write the answers on the board or overhead transparency so students can have the correct answers for study purposes. NOTE: It is a good practice in public speaking and leadership skills for individual students to take charge of leading the discussions of the study questions. Perhaps a different student could go to the front of the class and lead the discussion each day that the study questions are discussed during this unit. Of course, the teacher should guide the discussion when appropriate and be sure to fill in any gaps the students leave.

Activity #2
    Give students ten to fifteen minutes to look over the study questions and do the vocabulary work for Part II.

Activity #3
    Have students read Part II orally in class. Complete the oral reading evaluations. If students do not finish reading this section in class, they should do so prior to the next class period.

## ORAL READING EVALUATION - *Treasure Island*

Name _____ Class_____ Date _____

| SKILL | EXCELLENT | GOOD | AVERAGE | FAIR | POOR |
|---|---|---|---|---|---|
| Fluency | 5 | 4 | 3 | 2 | 1 |
| Clarity | 5 | 4 | 3 | 2 | 1 |
| Audibility | 5 | 4 | 3 | 2 | 1 |
| Pronunciation | 5 | 4 | 3 | 2 | 1 |
| _____ | 5 | 4 | 3 | 2 | 1 |
| _____ | 5 | 4 | 3 | 2 | 1 |

Total _____   Grade _____

Comments:

# LESSON FOUR

## Objectives
1. To review the main ideas and events from Part II
2. To do the prereading work for Part III
3. To read Part III
4. To introduce the Group Presentation Project

## Activity #1
Give students a few minutes to formulate answers for the study guide questions for Part II and then discuss the answers to the questions in detail. Write the answers on the board or overhead transparency so students can have the correct answers for study purposes.

## Activity #2
Tell students that prior to Lesson Six they should have completed the prereading and reading work for Part III. (Preview the study questions, do the vocabulary worksheet, and read the section.)

## Activity #3
Distribute the Group Presentation Project Assignment Sheet. Discuss the directions in detail. Divide your class into groups. If time remains in this class period, give students time to meet together in their groups to begin working on their projects.

# LESSON FIVE

## Objective
To give students time and resources to work on their group presentation projects

## Activity
Take students to your school's library/media center. Give students this class period to find information about their research topics. Remind students to fill out Nonfiction Reading Assignment Sheets for each of the nonfiction articles they read for this project to fulfill their nonfiction reading assignment for this unit.

# GROUP PRESENTATION PROJECT ASSIGNMENT SHEET - *Treasure Island*

## PROMPT

You are reading *Treasure Island*, a book about pirates and treasure hunting. What are the real facts about pirates and treasures, though? How much of this story is life-like, and how much is romanticized? You have been (or are about to be) divided into three large groups, one group for each of these topics: ships, pirates, and treasures.

## ASSIGNMENT

Your assignment is to prepare a 15-20 minute creative presentation about your topic.

You don't want to sit and listen to two boring, fifteen-minute presentations in which people just stand in front of the class and read from their research notes and neither does anyone else in the class. Therefore, you are required to make your presentations *creative*. Costumes, maps, pictures, video segments, diagrams, songs, models, etc. add so much to a presentation. Use whatever is appropriate to make the information you are presenting interesting.

Likewise, we don't want presentations that are all fluff and no *stuff*. You will be graded on *both* content *and* creativity.

## GETTING STARTED

***Ship Group:*** Your assignment is to tell us all about the ships of this era. How were they made? What kinds of ships were there? How many crew members would it take to manage the ship(s)? What were their jobs? How did the ships work? What were some common problems for seafaring folks? Tell us about food stores and supplies, living conditions, what it was really like to be on one of these ships, etc. There is a lot of information to research and report about on this topic. Divide the research load up among your group members so each person has at least one subtopic to research.

***Pirate Group***: Your assignment is to tell about *real* pirates. Who were some of the most infamous pirates in history? What did real pirates do? (Did they do all the things we read about or see in movies, or were they really much more benign?) What kinds of vessels did pirates most often attack? What did they do with the loot? How could vessels be protected against pirates? Are there still pirates on the seas today? Where or why not? Divide your group in half. Half of you should research real pirates (biographical information), and the other half of you should each take one other aspect of pirating to research.

***Treasure Group***: Your assignment is to tell about treasures, shipwrecks with treasures, and treasure hunting. What have been some of the greatest treasure finds in history? What are some of the most famous shipwrecks that were supposed to have had great treasures on board? Do people still hunt for treasures? If so, who, where and how? Divide your group into subgroups for each of these areas so a few of you will research each of these subtopics.

*Treasure Island* Group Presentation Project Assignment Sheet Page 2

## PLANNING THE PRESENTATION

After you have done the research, get together as a group and discuss what you have found; swap information so you can all have a clear idea of what information you have to present. After you have done this, then you can begin to work together to create your presentation.

Brainstorm ideas about how you could make an interesting presentation. Write them all down. When you can't think of anything else, go back and look at your list. Keep the best ideas--the ones that would be the most appropriate for your presentation--and decide what needs to be done for each prior to your presentation. Make a list of things that have to be done next to each idea you have chosen. Next to each thing that has to be done, write down who is to do it and by when it has to be done.

Finally, review the presentation plan as a group to make sure you are all in agreement as to what should be done, how it should be done, by whom it should be done, and by when it should be done.

## ON PRESENTATION DAY

You will not have much time to make preparations for your presentations on the presentation day. Therefore, have as much of your setting up work as possible done prior to class. For example, if you are planning to use costumes, get changed quickly before class starts. If you are using a video segment, have the video tape already wound to the proper place so you only have to plug it in to the video player. Make all the preparations you can prior to the beginning of class so you don't use up valuable presentation time during class.

## TIME

You will be given a class period to gather materials from the library/media center. You will also be given additional class time to work as a group planning your presentation. However, you will probably have to do some of your research and some of your preparation for the presentation outside of the regularly scheduled class periods.

## LESSON SIX

<u>Objectives</u>
    1. To review the main ideas and events from Part III
    2. To preview and read Part IV
    3. To give students time to work on their group projects

<u>Activity #1</u>
    Give students a few minutes to formulate answers to the study questions for Part III. Discuss students' answers in detail and write the "correct" answers on the board for students to copy for study use later.

<u>Activity #2</u>
    Tell students that prior to the next class period they should have completed the prereading and reading work for Part IV.

<u>Activity #3</u>
    Give students the remainder of this class period to work in their groups. They should finish gathering information and begin sharing the information they have found with other group members.

## LESSON SEVEN

<u>Objectives</u>
    1. To review the main ideas and events from Part IV
    2. To preview and read Part V
    3. To give students time to work on their group projects

<u>Activity #1</u>
    Give students a few minutes to formulate answers to the study questions for Part IV. Discuss students' answers in detail and write the "correct" answers on the board for students to copy for study use later.

<u>Activity #2</u>
    Tell students that prior to the next class period they should have completed the prereading and reading work for Part V.

<u>Activity #3</u>
    Give students the remainder of this class period to work in their groups. They should finish sharing information with other group members and begin creating their plans for their presentations.

## LESSON EIGHT

Objectives
- 1. To help students prepare for their group presentations
- 2. To give students the opportunity to practice writing to inform
- 3. To give the teacher the opportunity to evaluate progress of the group presentations and some idea as to what to expect for the presentation day

Activity
Distribute Writing Assignment #1. Discuss the directions in detail and give students ample time to complete the assignment.

## LESSON NINE

Objectives
- 1. To review the main ideas and events from Part V
- 2. To do the prereading work for Part VI
- 3. To read Part VI

Activity #1
Give students a few minutes to formulate answers for the study guide questions for Part V, and then discuss the answers to the questions in detail. Write the answers on the board or overhead transparency.

Activity #2
Give students ten to fifteen minutes to look over the study questions and do the vocabulary work for Part VI.

Activity #3
Have students read Part VI silently in class. If students do not finish reading this section in class, they should do so prior to the next class period.

# WRITING ASSIGNMENT #1 - *Treasure Island*

## PROMPT
In a few days you will have to give your group presentations. The purpose of this assignment is to help you prepare for your presentations. Your assignment is to write out your presentation plan.

## PREWRITING
A great deal of your prewriting has been done already through your research and your group planning sessions. Take a few minutes to review the plans you have made so far. Appoint one person as the group's secretary to write down the report of your plan.

## DRAFTING
Title your report "Group Presentation Plan: (fill in the name of your group)."

Make the first heading "Participants' Research." In this section, write down the names of the people in your group and next to their names, write down the subtopic(s) each was supposed to research.

Make the next heading "An Overview." In this section, give a brief overview of main points of information that will be covered in your presentation.

The next heading should be "The Details." In this section, explain *exactly* how you will do your presentation. For example, "To open our presentation, Sarah will show a 30-second film clip of the tall ships in New York's harbor for the American Bicentennial Celebration in 1976, giving a short narration introducing our topic--ships. Terry will then show a model of a three-masted ship circa 1760 while explaining how ships were constructed. . . . "

Make the next heading "Materials/Equipment Needed." State what, if any materials (such as projectors, etc.) you will need to have available in the room for your presentation.

The next heading should be "To Do." In this section, tell exactly what you have left to do to get your presentation together. Give specific tasks with specific names of people who have to do those tasks, and dates by which the tasks must be completed.

The final heading should be "Summary/Comments." This is your place to write down additional comments about your presentation and/or to summarize your presentation.

## PROMPT
When you finish the rough draft of your report, several group members should read it through to double-check your grammar, spelling, organization, and the clarity of your ideas.

# LESSON TEN

Objectives
1. To review the main ideas and events from Part VI
3. To discuss *Treasure Island* on interpretive and critical levels

Activity #1
Take a few minutes at the beginning of the period to review the study questions for Part VI.

Activity #2
Choose the questions from the Extra Discussion Questions/Writing Assignments which seem most appropriate for your students. A class discussion of these questions is most effective if students have been given the opportunity to formulate answers to the questions prior to the discussion. To this end, you may either have all the students formulate answers to all the questions, divide your class into groups and assign one or more questions to each group, or you could assign one question to each student in your class. The option you choose will make a difference in the amount of class time needed for this activity.

Activity #3
After students have had ample time to formulate answers to the questions, begin your class discussion of the questions and the ideas presented by the questions. Be sure students take notes during the discussion so they have information to study for the unit test.

# EXTRA WRITING ASSIGNMENTS/DISCUSSION QUESTIONS - *Treasure Island*

Interpretation

1. From what point of view is the story told? How does that affect our understanding of the story?

2. If you were to rewrite *Treasure Island* as a play, where would you start and end each act?

3. Are the characters in *Treasure Island* stereotypes? If so, explain why Robert Louis Stevenson used stereotypes. If not, explain how the characters merit individuality.

4. Where is the climax of the story? Justify your answer.

5. Explain the importance of the setting in *Treasure Island*. Could this story have been set in a different time and place and still have the same effect?

6. In what ways does Robert Louis Stevenson try to make the story believable? Is he successful; is the story believable?

7. What are the conflicts in the story, and how is each resolved?

Critical

8. Compare and contrast Bill Bones and John Silver.

9. What are Jim's good points and what are some of his faults?

10. Israel Hands said he had "no luck." Did he have any less luck than anyone else in the story, or was this just his way of making excuses for himself?

11. Characterize Robert Louis Stevenson's style of writing. How does it contribute to the value of the novel?

12. What characteristics of this story make it a great adventure tale?

13. Did John Silver have any redeeming qualities? What were his good characteristics?

14. Do any of the characters grow or change as a result of their adventures? If so, which ones, and how do they change? If not, why not?

15. What important things did Jim do during the times when he acted on his own? Why was each important to the ultimate success of the cruise?

16. What purpose(s) did the characters of Pew and Black Dog serve?

*Treasure Island* Extra Discussion Questions Page 2

Critical/Personal Response

17. Were Jim and Mrs. Hawkins right to take the oilcloth packet in the first place, or were they just as bad as the pirates?

18. Chapters 16 and 17 are narrated by the doctor. We have said that he narrated them so we could learn about events in which Jim did not directly participate. How else could this problem of narration have been resolved, and why do you think Mr. Stevenson chose to change narrators instead of handling it some other way? Why do you think he chose the doctor instead of one of the other characters?

19. Based on what you know about Jim, what do you think he did with his share of the money?

Personal Response

20. Did you enjoy reading *Treasure Island*? Why or why not?

21. Suppose the story had been written in the first person narrative from John Silver's point of view. How would it have been different?

22. If you were to find out about a treasure like Jim did, would you actually go looking for it like Jim did, or wouldn't you? Why?

23. What would you do with the money if you would find a treasure like Jim did?

24. Have you read other stories about pirates or treasure hunting? What were they? How do they compare to *Treasure Island*?

## LESSON ELEVEN

Objective
> To review all of the vocabulary work done in this unit

Activity
> Choose one (or more) of the vocabulary review activities listed below and spend your class period as directed in the activity. Some of the materials for these review activities are located in the Vocabulary Resource section of this unit.

### VOCABULARY REVIEW ACTIVITIES

1. Divide your class into two teams and have an old-fashioned spelling or definition bee.

2. Give each of your students (or students in groups of two, three or four) a *Treasure Island* Vocabulary Word Search Puzzle. The person (group) to find all of the vocabulary words in the puzzle first wins.

3. Give students a *Treasure Island* Vocabulary Word Search Puzzle without the word list. The person or group to find the most vocabulary words in the puzzle wins.

4. Use a *Treasure Island* Vocabulary Crossword Puzzle. Put the puzzle onto a transparency on the overhead projector (so everyone can see it), and do the puzzle together as a class.

5. Give students a *Treasure Island* Vocabulary Matching Worksheet to do.

6. Divide your class into two teams. Use the *Treasure Island* vocabulary words with their letters jumbled as a word list. Student 1 from Team A faces off against Student 1 from Team B. You write the first jumbled word on the board. The first student (1A or 1B) to unscramble the word wins the chance for his/her team to score points. If 1A wins the jumble, go to student 2A and give him/her a definition. He/she must give you the correct spelling of the vocabulary word which fits that definition. If he/she does, Team A scores a point, and you give student 3A a definition for which you expect a correctly spelled matching vocabulary word. Continue giving Team A definitions until some team member makes an incorrect response. An incorrect response sends the game back to the jumbled-word face off, this time with students 2A and 2B. Instead of repeating giving definitions to the first few students of each team, continue with the student after the one who gave the last incorrect response on the team. For example, if Team B wins the jumbled-word face-off, and student 5B gave the last incorrect answer for Team B, you would start this round of definition questions with student 6B, and so on. The team with the most points wins!

7. Have students write a story in which they correctly use as many vocabulary words as possible. Have students read their compositions orally! Post the most original compositions on your bulletin board!

## LESSON TWELVE

Objectives
    1. To educate students about ships, pirates, and treasures
    2. To bring the group projects to completion
    3. To give students the opportunity to practice public speaking
    4. To evaluate the group work

Activity
    Use this class period for the group presentations. You may need two class periods for this activity, depending upon the length of your class period and the length of your students' presentations. Use your own best judgment. The next lesson is a writing assignment, so if you need part of another class period, the writing activity can easily be started later in the class period.

## LESSON THIRTEEN

Objectives
    1. To give students the opportunity to practice writing to persuade
    2. To give the teacher the opportunity to evaluate students' writing skills
    3. To give students the opportunity to do some creative writing

Activity
    Distribute Writing Assignment #2. Discuss the directions orally in detail. Allow the remaining class time for students to complete the activity.


Follow-Up: After you have graded the assignments, have a writing conference with the students. After the writing conference, allow students to revise their papers using your suggestions and corrections. Give them about three days from the date they receive their papers to complete the revision. I suggest grading the revisions on an A-C-E scale (all revisions well-done, some revisions made, few or no revisions made). This will speed your grading time and still give some credit for the students' efforts.

# WRITING ASSIGNMENT #2 - *Treasure Island*

## PROMPT

Suppose you find a treasure map and you want to go hunting for the treasure. How would you go about doing that? Would you go to your parents and say, "Look, I found this cool treasure map, and I want to go find the treasure"? They would probably look at you like you were from Mars. Your assignment is to create a scenario in which you have found some kind of treasure map; the details of the finding and the map and the treasure are all left up to you. You are to write a composition in which you persuade your parent(s)/guardians to give you permission to go hunting for the treasure and for them to give you their support (by financing your trip and/or accompanying you).

## PREWRITING

First, work out the details of how you found the map, what kind of map it is, and what kind of a treasure is waiting to be found. Then add any other details to your scenario that you choose.

Make a list of reasons for and against the expedition. The reasons for the expedition are your reasons for wanting to go. The reasons against the expedition are probably reasons your parent(s) wouldn't want you to go (and are therefore objections to overcome with positive arguments). Next to each objection, write some notes as to how you might overcome the objection.

## DRAFTING

You have asked your parent(s) to sit down with you because you want to have a talk together. Your composition is a written version of what you would say to them during your talk together.

Write an introductory paragraph. How would you bring up the subject? This is a good place to explain how you found the map and the details of the validity of the find and of the treasure itself.

Write a paragraph for each of the reasons you want to go--each of the reasons *for* the expedition. Use a topic sentence for each of these paragraphs and fill out the paragraph with examples and facts that support your statements.

Write a paragraph for each of the objections--each of the reasons *against* the expedition-- in which you acknowledge the objections and offer your solution(s) or comments (if no solution is possible).

Write a concluding paragraph in which you summarize your ideas and make your final plea. By the time you get to this paragraph, there should be no doubt in your audience's (parents') mind that going on an expedition to find the treasure is the most advantageous thing to do.

## PROOFREADING

When you finish the rough draft of your paper, ask a student who sits near you to read it. After reading your rough draft, he/she should tell you what he/she liked best about your work, which parts were difficult to understand, and ways in which your work could be improved. Reread your paper considering your critic's comments and make the corrections you think are necessary. Do a final proofreading of your paper double-checking your grammar, spelling, organization, and the clarity of your ideas.

## LESSONS FOURTEEN AND FIFTEEN

Objectives
1. To show students a film interpretation of *Treasure Island*
2. To stimulate students' critical thinking
3. To reward students for all their good work during the unit

Activity

Show a film version of *Treasure Island*. Ask your students to pay particular attention to the movie to try to find any differences between the film version and the text. Also, tell students to take notes about the characters and scenes, about things they visualized differently as they read from how they appeared on the screen.

## LESSON SIXTEEN

Objectives
1. To give students the opportunity to practice writing their personal opinions
2. To review the book and the film versions of *Treasure Island*
3. To give the teacher a chance to evaluate students' writing skills

NOTE: Prior to this class period you need to find and bring in (or have students each bring in) one movie or book review from a newspaper or magazine.

Activity #1

Distribute several examples of movie and book review columns. Read through at least one with your students to show them the main elements in a movie and/or book review. Write down the main elements on the board or overhead for students to copy and follow for Writing Assignment #3.

Activity #2

Distribute Writing Assignment #3. Discuss the directions orally in detail. Allow the remaining class time for students to complete the activity.

NOTE: While students are working on Writing Assignment #3, call students to your desk (or some other private area) to discuss their papers from Writing Assignment #2. A Writing Evaluation Form is included with this unit to help structure your conferences.

Follow-Up: Follow up as in Writing Assignment #2, allowing students to correct their errors and turn in the revision for credit. A good time for your next writing conferences would be the day following the unit test.

## WRITING EVALUATION FORM - *Treasure Island*

Name _____ Date _____

Grade _____

Circle One For Each Item:

Grammar:        excellent      good    fair    poor

Spelling:       excellent      good    fair    poor

Punctuation:    excellent      good    fair    poor

Legibility:     excellent      good    fair   poor

_____

_____

Strengths:




Weaknesses:




Comments/Suggestions:

# WRITING ASSIGNMENT #3 - *Treasure Island*

## PROMPT

You have read the text of *Treasure Island*, and you have also seen a movie version of it. Now you are to turn into a professional critic and give your own views and opinions about the movie and the book. Your assignment is to write a column for a newspaper in which you review the movie and the book, *Treasure Island*.

## PREWRITING

You have read through at least one book or movie review and have discussed the main components of the review(s). Make a list of the main components on a piece of scratch paper. Next to each component, write what you would say about the movie. Next to that write what you would say about the book for the same component. Do that for each of the components.

| Component | Movie | Book |
|---|---|---|
| Plot | Jot down your thoughts about how well the movie reflected the same plot as the book. | Jot down your thoughts about the plot of the book. |
| Characters | Jot down your thoughts about how well the movie reflected the same characters as the book. | Jot down your thoughts about the characterization in the book. |

Continue your chart in this way.

## DRAFTING

Write a paragraph in which you give your opinion about the book and movie, *Treasure Island*.

Write one paragraph for each of the main components of a review. If you have a lot to say about each component, you may write two paragraphs for each component--one for the movie and one for the book. Use a topic sentence for each paragraph and use examples from the book or movie to support your statements.

Write a concluding paragraph in which you give your final thoughts about the book and movie of *Treasure Island*.

## PROOFREADING

When you finish the rough draft of your review, ask a student who sits near you to read it. After reading your rough draft, he/she should tell you what he/she liked best about your work, which parts were difficult to understand, and ways in which your work could be improved. Reread your paper considering your critic's comments and make the corrections you think are necessary. Do a final proofreading of your review double-checking your grammar, spelling, organization, and the clarity of your ideas.

# LESSON SEVENTEEN

<u>Objective</u>
To review the main ideas presented in *Treasure Island*

<u>Activity #1</u>
Choose one of the review games/activities included in this guide and spend your class period as outlined there. Some materials for these activities are located in the Extra Activities section of this unit.

<u>Activity #2</u>
Remind students that the Unit Test will be in the next class meeting. Stress the review of the Study Guides and their class notes as a last-minute, brush-up review for homework.

# REVIEW GAMES/ACTIVITIES - *Treasure Island*

1. Ask the class to make up a unit test for *Treasure Island*. The test should have 4 sections: matching, true/false, short answer, and essay. Students may use 1/2 period to make the test and then swap papers and use the other 1/2 class period to take a test a classmate has devised (open book). You may want to use the unit test included in this guide or take questions from the students' unit tests to formulate your own test.

2. Take 1/2 period for students to make up true and false questions (including the answers). Collect the papers and divide the class into two teams. Draw a big tick-tack-toe board on the chalk board. Make one team X and one team O. Ask questions to each side, giving each student one turn. If the question is answered correctly, that students' team's letter (X or O) is placed in the box. If the answer is incorrect, no mark is placed in the box. The object is to get three marks in a row like tick-tack-toe. You may want to keep track of the number of games won for each team.

3. Take 1/2 period for students to make up questions (true/false and short answer). Collect the questions. Divide the class into two teams. You'll alternate asking questions to individual members of teams A & B (like in a spelling bee). The question keeps going from A to B until it is correctly answered, then a new question is asked. A correct answer does not allow the team to get another question. Correct answers are +2 points; incorrect answers are -1 point.

4. Have students pair up and quiz each other from their study guides and class notes.

5. Give students a *Treasure Island* crossword puzzle to complete.

6. Divide your class into two teams. Use the *Treasure Island* crossword words with their letters jumbled as a word list. Student 1 from Team A faces off against Student 1 from Team B. You write the first jumbled word on the board. The first student (1A or 1B) to unscramble the word wins the chance for his/her team to score points. If 1A wins the jumble, go to student 2A and give him/her a clue. He/she must give you the correct word which matches that clue. If he/she does, Team A scores a point, and you give student 3A a clue for which you expect another correct response. Continue giving Team A clues until some team member makes an incorrect response. An incorrect response sends the game back to the jumbled-word face off, this time with students 2A and 2B. Instead of repeating giving clues to the first few students of each team, continue with the student after the one who gave the last incorrect response on the team. For example, if Team B wins the jumbled-word face-off, and student 5B gave the last incorrect answer for Team B, you would start this round of clue questions with student 6B, and so on. The team with the most points wins!

# UNIT TESTS

# SHORT ANSWER UNIT TEST 1 - *Treasure Island*

I. Matching

___ 1. Jim Hawkins       A. Buried the treasure

___ 2. Pew               B. Trelawney -- best shot of Smollett's group

___ 3. Israel Hands      C. Captain of the ship going to Treasure Island

___ 4. Bill Bones        D. Hawkins' inn

___ 5. Livesey           E. "Man of the Island"

___ 6. Squire            F. First of Smollett's men to die

___ 7. John Silver       G. Missing 2 fingers; saved by a wooden sign

___ 8. Black Dog         H. Magistrate and doctor

___ 9. Ben Gunn          I. Ship that went to Treasure Island

___ 10. Flint            J. Peg-legged cook and pirate

___ 11. Admiral Benbow   K. Blind buccaneer

___ 12. Smollett         L. Boy narrator

___ 13. Redruth          M. Had Jim watch out for a man with a wooden leg

___ 14. Hispaniola       N. Jim killed him

*Treasure Island* Short Answer Unit Test 1 Page 2

II. Short Answer

1. How did Jim and Mrs. Hawkins discover the map?

2. Why didn't Jim think Long John Silver was a pirate when he first met him?

3. What did Jim hear while he was in the apple barrel?

4. Why did the captain give the men an afternoon ashore when they arrived at the island?

5. What did Jim's group decide would be their "best hope" for survival?

6. What truce offer did Long John Silver make to Captain Smollett, and what was Smollett's response?

*Treasure Island* Short Answer Unit Test 1 Page 3

7. What was Jim's "second folly"?

8. How did Silver get possession of the blockhouse?

9. Why did the council decide to invalidate the black spot and keep Silver as captain?

10. What surprise did Silver and the pirates find at the treasure site?

11. What happened to Silver?

12. What happened to the treasure?

*Treasure Island* Short Answer Unit Test 1 Page 4

III. Essay

*Treasure Island* is considered a "classic" work of literature. Give your opinion as to why it is considered a classic. Thoroughly explain your answer using paragraph form and your best written English.

*Treasure Island* Short Answer Unit Test 1 Page 5

IV. Vocabulary

>Listen to the vocabulary words and write them down. After you have spelled all the words, go back and write down the definitions.

1.

2.

3.

4.

5.

6.

7.

8.

9.

10.

# SHORT ANSWER UNIT TEST 2 - *Treasure Island*

I. Matching

___ 1. Jim Hawkins     A. Trelawney -- best shot of Smollett's group

___ 2. Pew     B. Captain of the ship going to Treasure Island

___ 3. Israel Hands     C. Buried the treasure

___ 4. Bill Bones     D. "Man of the Island"

___ 5. Livesey     E. First of Smollett's men to die

___ 6. Squire     F. Missing 2 fingers; saved by a wooden sign

___ 7. John Silver     G. Hawkins' inn

___ 8. Black Dog     H. Jim killed him

___ 9. Ben Gunn     I. Had Jim watch out for a man with a wooden leg

___ 10. Flint     J. Blind buccaneer

___ 11. Admiral Benbow     K. Boy narrator

___ 12. Smollett     L. Peg-legged cook and pirate

___ 13. Redruth     M. Ship that went to Treasure Island

___ 14. Hispaniola     N. Magistrate and doctor

*Treasure Island* Short Answer Unit Test 2 Page 2

II. Short Answer
1. Why did Captain Bill Bones come to the Admiral Benbow?


2. Why didn't Captain Bill Bones kill Black Dog?


3. Why did Jim and Mrs. Hawkins go to the neighboring hamlet after Captain Bones' death?


4. What did Jim hear while he was in the apple barrel?


5. What did Jim witness from his hiding place in the thicket?


6. What message was Jim to deliver to the squire or the doctor for Ben Gunn?

*Treasure Island* Short Answer Unit Test 2 Page 3

7. What truce offer did Long John Silver make to Captain Smollett, and what was Smollett's response?

8. What deal did Israel Hands make with Jim?

9. How did Silver get possession of the blockhouse?

10. Why did the council decide to invalidate the black spot and keep Silver as captain?

11. Who got the treasure?

12. What happened to Silver?

*Treasure Island* Short Answer Unit Test 2 Page 4

III. Composition
    Robert Louis Stevenson wrote *Treasure Island* when his stepson asked him to write "something really interesting." Explain in what ways *Treasure Island* fulfills this request.

*Treasure Island* Short Answer Unit Test 2 Page 5

IV. Vocabulary

> Listen to the vocabulary words and write them down. After you have spelled all the words, go back and write down the definitions.

1.

2.

3.

4.

5.

6.

7.

8.

9.

10.

# KEY: SHORT ANSWER UNIT TESTS - *Treasure Island*

The short answer questions are taken directly from the study guides.
If you need to look up the answers, you will find them in the study guide section.

Answers to the composition questions will vary depending on your
class discussions and the level of your students.

For the vocabulary section of the test, choose ten of the
words from the vocabulary lists to read orally for your students.

The answers to the matching section of the test are below.

Answers to the matching section of the Advanced Short Answer Unit Test
are the same as for Short Answer Unit Test #2.

| Test #1 | Test #2 |
|---|---|
| 1. L | 1. M |
| 2. K | 2. J |
| 3. N | 3. H |
| 4. M | 4. I |
| 5. H | 5. N |
| 6. B | 6. A |
| 7. J | 7. L |
| 8. G | 8. F |
| 9. E | 9. D |
| 10. A | 10. C |
| 11. D | 11. G |
| 12. C | 12. B |
| 13. F | 13. E |
| 14. I | 14. M |

# ADVANCED SHORT ANSWER UNIT TEST - *Treasure Island*

I. Matching

___  1. Jim Hawkins         A. Trelawney -- best shot of Smollett's group

___  2. Pew                 B. Captain of the ship going to Treasure Island

___  3. Israel Hands        C. Buried the treasure

___  4. Bill Bones          D. "Man of the Island"

___  5. Livesey             E. First of Smollett's men to die

___  6. Squire              F. Missing 2 fingers; saved by a wooden sign

___  7. John Silver         G. Hawkins' inn

___  8. Black Dog           H. Jim killed him

___  9. Ben Gunn            I. Had Jim watch out for a man with a wooden leg

___ 10. Flint               J. Blind buccaneer

___ 11. Admiral Benbow      K. Boy narrator

___ 12. Smollett            L. Peg-legged cook and pirate

___ 13. Redruth             M. Ship that went to Treasure Island

___ 14. Hispaniola          N. Magistrate and doctor

*Treasure Island* Advanced Short Answer Unit Test Page 2

II. Short Answer

1. Compare and contrast Bill Bones and John Silver.

2. Did John Silver have any redeeming qualities? What were his good characteristics, and what were his faults?

3. From what point of view was the story told? What effect did that have on the story?

4. Was Ben Gunn necessary to the story? Why was he included?

*Treasure Island* Advanced Short Answer Unit Test Page 3

III. Essay

Choose any four characters and explain how each one contributes to the excitement and adventure in *Treasure Island*.

*Treasure Island* Advanced Short Answer Unit Test Page 4

IV. Vocabulary

    Listen to the vocabulary words and write them down. Go back later and write a composition using all of the words. The composition must in some way relate to *Treasure Island*.

# MULTIPLE CHOICE UNIT TEST 1 - *Treasure Island*

I. Matching

___  1. Jim Hawkins            A. Buried the treasure

___  2. Pew                    B. Trelawney -- best shot of Smollett's group

___  3. Israel Hands           C. Captain of the ship going to Treasure Island

___  4. Bill Bones             D. Hawkins' inn

___  5. Livesey                E. "Man of the Island"

___  6. Squire                 F. First of Smollett's men to die

___  7. John Silver            G. Missing 2 fingers; saved by a wooden sign

___  8. Black Dog              H. Magistrate and doctor

___  9. Ben Gunn               I. Ship that went to Treasure Island

___ 10. Flint                  J. Peg-legged cook and pirate

___ 11. Admiral Benbow         K. Blind buccaneer

___ 12. Smollett               L. Boy narrator

___ 13. Redruth                M. Had Jim watch out for a man with a wooden leg

___ 14. Hispaniola             N. Jim killed him

*Treasure Island* Multiple Choice Unit Test 1 Page 2

II. Multiple Choice

1. Why did Captain Bill Bones come to the inn?
   a. He was recovering from a bad case of scurvy and had orders from his doctor to rest.
   b. He was looking for a comfortable out-of-the-way place to stay where the other pirates couldn't find him and the treasure map.
   c. He wanted to assemble a crew to go and find the treasure.
   d. He was hoping to buy the inn and become a respectable innkeeper.

2. Which of the following statements is true concerning the captain's presence at the inn?
   a. Mr. Hawkins and Jim both thought it was a bad idea to have him there because he would frighten other people away.
   b. Jim thought it was a bad idea because the captain was noisy and rude, but Mr. Hawkins wanted the money.
   c. Mr. Hawkins thought it was bad because the captain would frighten people away, but Jim thought it might be good because people enjoyed the captain's stories, even if they were scared of him.
   d. Both of them thought it was good for business to have such a character around, but Jim's mother was afraid of him and said he could not stay.

3. For what reason did Pew come to see Captain Bill Bones?
   a. To buy the treasure map
   b. To blackmail him
   c. To kill him
   d. To give him the black spot, his death notice

4. Why did the captain give the men an afternoon ashore when they arrived at the island?
   a. He needed time to rest himself because he had been sick on the voyage.
   b. He needed time to think about what to do.
   c. He wanted to give Long John Silver the opportunity to talk to the men and get them in order to avoid mutiny as long as possible.
   d. He was planning to steal the ship and sail back home without them.

5. What did Jim witness from his hiding place in the thicket?
   a. He saw Long John Silver kill Tom, a mate who would have been loyal to Captain Smollett.
   b. He saw Captain Smollett throwing supplies overboard.
   c. He saw two of the crewmen putting a hole in the bottom of the rowboat.
   d. He saw Mr. Arrow giving a piece of paper and a handful of coins to Long John Silver.

6. What did Jim's group decide would be their best hope for survival?
   a. They would go back to the ship and try to sail away.
   b. They would burn down all of the vegetation on the island to expose the buccaneers.
   c. They would kill as many of the buccaneers as possible and use their supplies to survive.
   d. They would try to make a deal with the buccaneers to split all of the profits when they found the treasure.

*Treasure Island* Multiple Choice Unit Test 1 Page 3

7. After the *Hispaniola* was set adrift, Jim boarded her. Why did he do this?
   a. He wanted to get more food supplies.
   b. He was looking for extra weapons and gunpowder.
   c. It seemed as though no one was sailing her, and he hoped to return her to Captain Smollett.
   d. He had decided to set her afire so that the buccaneers would not be able to use her at all.

8. How did Israel Hands die?
   a. Jim had poisoned the wine. Israel drank it and died almost immediately.
   b. He lunged at Jim, who ducked. The momentum carried Israel overboard.
   c. Jim had been able to sneak around behind Hands. He told Hands to put down the knife and turn around. When Hands refused, Jim shot him.
   d. When he threw his knife at Jim, pinning him by the shoulder to the mast, both of Jim's pistols went off, and Hands plunged into the water.

9. What was Jim's deal with Silver?
   a. Jim only wanted safe passage home. He promised he would never speak of the search for the treasure.
   b. If Silver would spare his life, Jim would stand up for Silver in court and do all he could to save his life.
   c. Jim wanted to join the buccaneers. He thought that if he acted like one of Silver's men, he would have a better chance of escaping at a later time.
   d. Jim asked to be left on the island and for Silver to send a rescue ship after him.

10. What surprise did Silver and the pirates find at the treasure site?
    a. The treasure had already been found and removed.
    b. There was twice as much treasure as they had expected.
    c. There was a flag with a skull and crossbones with a written warning.
    d. The treasure was booby-trapped.

11. Who got the treasure?
    a. Silver had found it and hidden it.
    b. Jim had taken it aboard the *Hispaniola*.
    c. Ben Gunn had found it and stored it away before the *Hispaniola* had arrived.
    d. The doctor had managed to get it and hide it on the other side of the island.

12. What happened to Silver?
    a. He returned to Bristol, was tried, and spent the rest of his life in prison.
    b. He escaped from the ship at the first port they found in Spanish America, taking a sack of treasure with him.
    c. He killed himself, saying it was preferable to a life in prison.
    d. He escaped when they reached Bristol, saying he would spend the rest of his life hunting them down and seeking revenge.

III. Composition
   Is the story of *Treasure Island* believable? If so, what things make it believable? If not, why isn't it?

*Treasure Island* Multiple Choice Unit Test 1 Page 5

IV. Vocabulary - Match the correct definitions to the words.

____ 1. CONSORT          A. State of being alone; seclusion

____ 2. SOLITUDE         B. A hint; a slight knowledge or vague notion

____ 3. COGNAC           C. A ship keeping company with another

____ 4. APOPLEXY         D. Echoes of sound

____ 5. BOATSWAIN        E. A cart rope; a trace or part of a harness

____ 6. BYGONES          F. A stroke caused by a rupture of an artery of the brain

____ 7. BEFALL           G. To skip with a glancing rebound or series of rebounds

____ 8. BILLOWS          H. Muskets; firearms

____ 9. WAINROPES        I. Fawning; obedient; compliant

____ 10. ADMIXTURE       J. That which is added to anything by mixing

____ 11. OBSEQUIOUS      K. Narrow strips to form the sides of a barrel; to break a hole in; to ward off

____ 12. REPUGNANCE      L. Until now

____ 13. STAVE           M. Officer on a ship in charge of rigging & cables

____ 14. HITHERTO        N. Linger or delay

____ 15. REVERBERATIONS  O. To happen to

____ 16. MUSKETRY        P. A superior French brandy

____ 17. DESPERADOES     Q. Past; things gone by

____ 18. TARRY           R. Great waves or surges of water

____ 19. INKLING         S. Desperate criminals

____ 20. RICOCHET        T. Aversion; loathing; disdain

# MULTIPLE CHOICE UNIT TEST 2 - *Treasure Island*

I. Matching

___ 1. Jim Hawkins            A. Trelawney -- best shot of Smollett's group

___ 2. Pew                    B. Captain of the ship going to Treasure Island

___ 3. Israel Hands           C. Buried the treasure

___ 4. Bill Bones             D. "Man of the Island"

___ 5. Livesey                E. First of Smollett's men to die

___ 6. Squire                 F. Missing 2 fingers; saved by a wooden sign

___ 7. John Silver            G. Hawkins' inn

___ 8. Black Dog              H. Jim killed him

___ 9. Ben Gunn               I. Had Jim watch out for a man with a wooden leg

___ 10. Flint                 J. Blind buccaneer

___ 11. Admiral Benbow        K. Boy narrator

___ 12. Smollett              L. Peg-legged cook and pirate

___ 13. Redruth               M. Ship that went to Treasure Island

___ 14. Hispaniola            N. Magistrate and doctor

*Treasure Island* Multiple Choice Unit Test 1 Page 2

II. Multiple Choice

1. Why did Captain Bill Bones come to the inn?
    a. He wanted to assemble a crew to go and find the treasure.
    b. He was hoping to buy the inn and become a respectable innkeeper.
    c. He was recovering from a bad case of scurvy and had orders from his doctor to rest.
    d. He was looking for a comfortable out-of-the-way place to stay where the other pirates couldn't find him and the treasure map.

2. Which of the following statements is true concerning the captain's presence at the inn?
    a. Mr. Hawkins thought it was bad because the captain would frighten people away, but Jim thought it might be good because people enjoyed the captain's stories, even if they were scared of him.
    b. Both of them thought it was good for business to have such a character around, but Jim's mother was afraid of him and said he could not stay.
    c. Mr. Hawkins and Jim both thought it was a bad idea to have him there because he would frighten other people away.
    d. Jim thought it was a bad idea because the captain was noisy and rude, but Mr. Hawkins wanted the money.

3. For what reason did Pew come to see Captain Bill Bones?
    a. To blackmail him
    b. To give him the Black Spot, his death notice
    c. To buy the treasure map
    d. To kill him

4. Why did the captain give the men an afternoon ashore when they arrived at the island?
    a. He needed time to rest himself because he had been sick on the voyage.
    b. He wanted to give Long John Silver the opportunity to talk to the men and get them in order to avoid mutiny as long as possible.
    c. He was planning to steal the ship and sail back home without them.
    d. He needed time to think about what to do.

5. What did Jim witness from his hiding place in the thicket?
    a. He saw Captain Smollett throwing supplies overboard.
    b. He saw two of the crewmen putting a hole in the bottom of the rowboat.
    c. He saw Long John Silver kill Tom, a mate who would have been loyal to Captain Smollett.
    d. He saw Mr. Arrow giving a piece of paper and a handful of coins to Long John Silver.

6. What did Jim's group decide would be their best hope for survival?
    a. They would kill as many of the buccaneers as possible and use their supplies to survive.
    b. They would burn down all of the vegetation on the island to expose the buccaneers.
    c. They would try to make a deal with the buccaneers to split all of the profits when they found the treasure.
    d. They would go back to the ship and try to sail away.

*Treasure Island* Multiple Choice Unit Test 1 Page 3

7. After the *Hispaniola* was set adrift, Jim boarded her. Why did he do this?
    a. He had decided to set her afire so that the buccaneers would not be able to use her at all.
    b. It seemed as though no one was sailing her, and he hoped to return her to Captain Smollett.
    c. He wanted to get more food supplies.
    d. He was looking for extra weapons and gunpowder.

8. How did Israel Hands die?
    a. Jim had been able to sneak around behind Hands. He told Hands to put down the knife and turn around. When Hands refused, Jim shot him.
    b. He lunged at Jim, who ducked. The momentum carried Israel overboard.
    c. Jim had poisoned the wine. Israel drank it and died almost immediately.
    d. When he threw his knife at Jim, pinning him by the shoulder to the mast, both of Jim's pistols went off, and Hands plunged into the water.

9. What was Jim's deal with Silver?
    a. If Silver would spare his life, Jim would stand up for Silver in court and do all he could to save his life.
    b. Jim only wanted safe passage home. He promised he would never speak of the search for the treasure.
    c. Jim asked to be left on the island and for Silver to send a rescue ship after him.
    d. Jim wanted to join the buccaneers. He thought that if he acted like one of Silver's men, he would have a better chance of escaping at a later time.

10. What surprise did Silver and the pirates find at the treasure site?
    a. The treasure was booby-trapped.
    b. There was a flag with a skull and crossbones with a written warning.
    c. The treasure had already been found and removed.
    d. There was twice as much treasure as they had expected.

11. Who got the treasure?
    a. Jim had taken it aboard the *Hispaniola*.
    b. Ben Gunn had found it and stored it away before the *Hispaniola* had arrived.
    c. Silver had found it and hidden it.
    d. The doctor had managed to get it and hide it on the other side of the island.

12. What happened to Silver?
    a. He killed himself, saying it was preferable to a life in prison.
    b. He escaped when they reached Bristol, saying he would spend the rest of his life hunting them down and seeking revenge.
    c. He returned to Bristol, was tried, and spent the rest of his life in prison.
    d. He escaped from the ship at the first port they found in Spanish America, taking a sack of treasure with him.

*Treasure Island* Multiple Choice Unit Test 1 Page 4

III. Composition

1. Compare and contrast Bill Bones and John Silver.

2. Compare and contrast Dr. Livesey and the squire.

3. Is Ben Gunn a "good guy" or a "bad guy"? Defend your answer.

*Treasure Island* Multiple Choice Unit Test 1 Page 5

IV. Vocabulary - Match the correct definitions to the words.

| | | |
|---|---|---|
| ____ 1. ACQUIESCENCE | | A. Narrow strips to form the sides of a barrel; to break a hole in; to ward off |
| ____ 2. STAVE | | B. A ship keeping company with another |
| ____ 3. SCOUR | | C. A cavalry sword with a somewhat curved blade |
| ____ 4. SABRE | | D. A hint; a slight knowledge or vague notion |
| ____ 5. TEETOTUM | | E. Kind of gallows on which malefactors were hung in chains and allowed to remain there as a warning |
| ____ 6. OBSEQUIOUS | | F. Pirates |
| ____ 7. GROG | | G. Officer on a ship in charge of rigging & cables |
| ____ 8. WAINROPES | | H. Moving up and down or backward and forward |
| ____ 9. GIBBET | | I. Simultaneous discharge of arrows, bullets, etc. |
| ____ 10. APOPLEXY | | J. A cruel, brutal person |
| ____ 11. INKLING | | K. To make clean & bright by friction; to clear away; diarrhea in cattle |
| ____ 12. UNDULATING | | L. A small opening through which small arms may be discharged |
| ____ 13. BOATSWAIN | | M. A person of distinction |
| ____ 14. LOOPHOLE | | N. Fawning; obedient; compliant |
| ____ 15. RUFFIAN | | O. Foolishness |
| ____ 16. BUCCANEERS | | P. A stroke caused by a rupture of an artery of the brain |
| ____ 17. FOLLY | | Q. Act of complying passively without implying agreement |
| ____ 18. CONSORT | | R. A cart rope; a trace or part of a harness |
| ____ 19. PERSONAGE | | S. A child's toy somewhat like a top |
| ____ 20. VOLLEY | | T. Any intoxicating liquor |

## ANSWER SHEET - *Treasure Island*
## Multiple Choice Unit Tests

| I. Matching | II. Multiple Choice | IV. Vocabulary |
|---|---|---|
| 1. ___ | 1. ___ | 1. ___ |
| 2. ___ | 2. ___ | 2. ___ |
| 3. ___ | 3. ___ | 3. ___ |
| 4. ___ | 4. ___ | 4. ___ |
| 5. ___ | 5. ___ | 5. ___ |
| 6. ___ | 6. ___ | 6. ___ |
| 7. ___ | 7. ___ | 7. ___ |
| 8. ___ | 8. ___ | 8. ___ |
| 9. ___ | 9. ___ | 9. ___ |
| 10. ___ | 10. ___ | 10. ___ |
| 11. ___ | 11. ___ | 11. ___ |
| 12. ___ | 12. ___ | 12. ___ |
| 13. ___ | | 13. ___ |
| 14. ___ | | 14. ___ |
| | | 15. ___ |
| | | 16. ___ |
| | | 17. ___ |
| | | 18. ___ |
| | | 19. ___ |
| | | 20. ___ |

# ANSWER KEY - *Treasure Island*
## Multiple Choice Unit Tests

Answers to Unit Test 1 are in the left column. Answers to Unit Test 2 are in the right column.

| I. Matching | II. Multiple Choice | IV. Vocabulary |
|---|---|---|
| 1. L  K | 1. B  D | 1. C  Q |
| 2. K  J | 2. C  A | 2. A  A |
| 3. N  H | 3. D  B | 3. P  K |
| 4. M  I | 4. C  B | 4. F  C |
| 5. H  N | 5. A  C | 5. M  S |
| 6. B  A | 6. C  A | 6. Q  N |
| 7. J  L | 7. C  B | 7. O  T |
| 8. G  F | 8. D  D | 8. R  R |
| 9. E  D | 9. B  A | 9. E  E |
| 10. A  C | 10. A  C | 10. J  P |
| 11. D  G | 11. C  B | 11. I  D |
| 12. C  B | 12. D  D | 12. T  H |
| 13. F  E |  | 13. K  G |
| 14. I  M |  | 14. L  L |
|  |  | 15. D  J |
|  |  | 16. H  F |
|  |  | 17. S  O |
|  |  | 18. N  B |
|  |  | 19. B  M |
|  |  | 20. G  I |

# UNIT RESOURCE MATERIALS

# BULLETIN BOARD IDEAS - *Treasure Island*

1. Save one corner of the board for the best of students' *Treasure Island* writing assignments.

2. Use the bulletin board from Lesson One as your bulletin board.

3. Title the board PIRATES OF THE PAST. Post biographies of infamous pirates.

4. Take one of the word search puzzles from the resource section and with a marker copy it over in a large size on the bulletin board. Write the clue words to find to one side. Invite students prior to and after class to find the words and circle them on the bulletin board.

5. Draw a big map of the island with the many points noted in the book located on the map. Make a cut-out *Hispaniola* to place in the water, etc.

6. Make a bulletin board about careers in the ship building industry, medicine, law, hotel/motel business, etc.

7. Write several of the most significant quotations from the book onto the board on brightly colored paper.

8. Make a bulletin board listing the vocabulary words for this unit. As you complete sections of the novel and discuss the vocabulary for each section, write the definitions on the bulletin board. (If your board is one students face frequently, it will help them learn the words.)

9. Make a bulletin board relating to survival skills. Perhaps your guest speaker could help provide some materials.

# EXTRA ACTIVITIES

One of the difficulties in teaching a novel is that all students don't read at the same speed. One student who likes to read may take the book home and finish it in a day or two. Sometimes a few students finish the in-class assignments early. The problem, then, is finding suitable extra activities for students.

The best thing I've found is to keep a little library in the classroom. For this unit on *Treasure Island*, you might check out from the school library other related books and articles about survival skills, treasure hunting, remote islands, pirates, or adventure stories. Articles of criticism about *Treasure Island*, the text or the movie, would be interesting for some students. Biographical information about the author or other works by the author would also be good to have on hand.

Other things you may keep on hand are puzzles. We have made some relating directly to *Treasure Island* for you. Feel free to duplicate them for your class.

Some students may like to draw. You might devise a contest or allow some extra-credit grade for students who draw characters or scenes from *Treasure Island*. Note, too, that if the students do not want to keep their drawings you may pick up some extra bulletin board materials this way. If you have a contest and you supply the prize (a CD or something like that perhaps), you could possibly make the drawing itself a non-refundable entry fee.

The pages which follow contain games, puzzles and worksheets. The keys, when appropriate, immediately follow the puzzle or worksheet. There are two main groups of activities: one group for the unit; that is, generally relating to the *Treasure Island* text, and another group of activities related strictly to the *Treasure Island* vocabulary.

Directions for these games, puzzles and worksheets are self-explanatory. The object here is to provide you with extra materials you may use in any way you choose.

# MORE ACTIVITIES - *Treasure Island*

1. Pick a chapter or scene with a great deal of dialogue and have the students act it out on a stage. (Perhaps you could assign various scenes to different groups of students so more than one scene could be acted and more students could participate.)

2. Divide your students into six groups. Have each group rewrite one part of the book as a play, assign parts, design costumes, and perform their parts of the play for the remainder of the class.

3. Have students create a game in which they use the settings and the characters from *Treasure Island*.

4. Have students design a book cover (front and back and inside flaps) for *Treasure Island*.

5. Have students design a bulletin board (ready to be put up, not just sketched) for *Treasure Island*.

6. Have students research and report on any of the topics listed for suggested extra reading.

7. Have students write a Captain's Log for the journey, told from Captain Smollett's point of view.

8. Have small groups of students design a board game called TREASURE ISLAND. They must write out the rules and make a prototype of the game which could actually be played.

9. Explain to your students the various ranks which can be held by naval officers. Have all of your students start out at the lowest rank. Work out a scale by which earning points for their various assignments during the unit they can reach the rank of Admiral (or a lesser rank if they do not do well or don't cooperate in class). Post each student's rank next to his name on the bulletin board or some other place in the room.

10. A variation of #9 would be to make a map with various points marked along the way to a treasure. As students accumulate points for good grades, attendance, etc., they advance towards the treasure and are rewarded with some treasure of your choice when they reach it.

11. Have each student hide a treasure in the school and write directions to the treasure--make a treasure map. Have students swap maps and find each other's treasures.

# WORD SEARCH - *Treasure Island*

All words in this list are associated with *Treasure Island*. The words are placed backwards, forward, diagonally, up and down. The included words are listed below the word searches.

```
S B T B S S Z E D D T L V K M C K Y H P D D N F
Q Y L Z Y E V N C E D M M X J P W V L A X V B C
Y L C A D O T G D R Z W U P I P J D A D M J K S
M A S T C O R A C L E C U R T N I L F B I L L Y
Q A M D B K K W M P W W A R F H O B Y V O V E D
S H P B S C D R W Y Q T Q L A I S P P T Y L Z T
S T O W O T R O P Z E N I W N N Y I S S H I P H
W L E T S N B Q G Y H M K A C W S I L T R B V J
I T S V X N E M R T E I P T T L R P O V B T G Q
Z S L D E F X S J H N S Y T A B X L E T E S R V
J V R B N N U G M S I B E N A N C H O R X R M K
V O T A L A S N T H T L D V I L X L T B I I S B
H F L T E A H O L V L S L S I T R X G U J U H V
J X V L F L C T N O D J C O J L U F F J R R Q J
L Z H C Y Y V K M T R E A S U R E M Z K C D P S
H K G F J R V S S Y K Z P S G C Z L J Q D R E W
D W P R X W O J N P R K G C G R Y B H C F Q Q R
R B V C L R N G V G O L M G W J J S B N D X C V
D J H S T W B L E T V T R S Q Y Y W R M N Z R F
C G K D S V N Y S R P K F S B X L F F R P L D T
```

| ANCHOR | FLINT | LIVESEY | SHIP |
| BEN | GUN | MAP | SILVER |
| BENBOW | GUNN | MAST | SMOLLETT |
| BILL | HAMLET | MATES | SQUIRE |
| BLACKDOG | HANDS | MUTINY | STEVENSON |
| BLACKSPOT | HAWKINS | OILCLOTH | STOCKADE |
| BONES | HISPANIOLA | PEW | STOW |
| BRISTOL | ISLAND | PIRATE | TREASURE |
| CORACLE | ISRAEL | PORT | TRUCE |
| COVE | JIM | REDRUTH | WINE |
| CREW | JOLLYROGER | RUM | |

# CROSSWORD *Treasure Island*

# CROSSWORD CLUES - *Treasure Island*

## ACROSS
1. Man of the Island
2. Jim cut the Hispaniola's
5. Protected waters
8. Pirate flag
10. Magistrate and doctor
12. When seas are not stormy they are ---
14. Buried the treasure
15. Bill ____
17. Myself
19. Shows where the treasure is
20. Big boat; sea transport
22. Jim & his mother went to the neighboring ____
23. Inquire
25. Making use of
26. Pirates' drink
28. Places where boats tie up in slips
29. ____ away; hide
30. Bristol, for example; city place where ships dock
31. Ingest food
32. Israel ____
33. Fuel often used for lamps in olden days
36. Opposite of old
37. Not pretty
39. A white flag is a sign of this
40. Belonging to me
42. Edge of a continent or island
43. Buccaneer
44. Coordinating conjunction
45. Trelawney; best shot of Smollett's group
46. Death notice

## DOWN
1. Told Jim to watch for a man with a wooden leg
3. Ben's boat
4. Contained the map
5. Those who work on the ship
6. Jim's home port
7. Admiral ____: the Hawkins' inn
8. Boy narrator
9. The long nine was one
11. Name of the ship that went to Treasure Island
13. Treasure ____
16. Hands on a ship
18. Missing two fingers; saved by a wooden sign
19. Tall pole on a ship
20. Captain Long John ____
21. Jim killed him
24. Capt. of ship going to Treasure Island
27. When the mates overthrow the captain
29. Blockhouse where Smollett's men stayed for a while
32. Jim's last name
34. Ben ____
35. Blind buccaneer
38. Side away from the wind
41. Affirmative reply

## CROSSWORD ANSWER KEY - *Treasure Island*

# MATCHING QUIZ/WORKSHEET 1 - *Treasure Island*

\_\_\_\_ 1. ISLAND               A. Treasure \_\_\_\_

\_\_\_\_ 2. BENBOW              B. Buccaneer

\_\_\_\_ 3. MATES                C. Pirates' drink

\_\_\_\_ 4. FLINT                D. Magistrate and doctor

\_\_\_\_ 5. CORACLE              E. Hands on a ship

\_\_\_\_ 6. ISRAEL               F. Jim's home port

\_\_\_\_ 7. PEW                  G. Pirate flag

\_\_\_\_ 8. JOLLYROGER           H. The long nine was one

\_\_\_\_ 9. RUM                  I. Ben's boat

\_\_\_\_ 10. BRISTOL             J. Protected waters

\_\_\_\_ 11. PORT                K. Blind buccaneer

\_\_\_\_ 12. PIRATE              L. Israel \_\_\_\_

\_\_\_\_ 13. BLACKDOG            M. Boy narrator

\_\_\_\_ 14. COVE                N. Buried the treasure

\_\_\_\_ 15. HANDS               O. Missing two fingers; saved by a wooden sign

\_\_\_\_ 16. JIM                 P. Bristol, for example; city place where ships dock

\_\_\_\_ 17. HAMLET              Q. Jim & his mother went to the neighboring \_\_\_

\_\_\_\_ 18. GUN                 R. Jim killed him

\_\_\_\_ 19. STOCKADE            S. Blockhouse where Smollett's men stayed for a while

\_\_\_\_ 20. LIVESEY             T. Admiral \_\_\_\_: the Hawkins' inn

# MATCHING QUIZ/WORKSHEET 2 - *Treasure Island*

____ 1. COVE           A. Captain Long John ____

____ 2. BRISTOL        B. Buried the treasure

____ 3. PORT           C. Protected waters

____ 4. TREASURE       D. Jim's home port

____ 5. PIRATE         E. Blind buccaneer

____ 6. GUNN           F. Name of the ship that went to Treasure Island

____ 7. BLACKDOG       G. Buccaneer

____ 8. BEN            H. Shows where the treasure is

____ 9. LIVESEY        I. ____ Island

____ 10. SHIP          J. Death notice

____ 11. FLINT         K. Contained the map

____ 12. SILVER        L. Big boat; sea transport

____ 13. WINE          M. Missing two fingers; saved by a wooden sign

____ 14. OILCLOTH      N. Man of the Island

____ 15. STOW          O. ___ away; hide

____ 16. PEW           P. Ben ____

____ 17. CORACLE       Q. What Hands wanted Jim to get

____ 18. BLACKSPOT     R. Bristol, for example; city place where ships dock

____ 19. MAP           S. Ben's boat

____ 20. HISPANIOLA    T. Magistrate and doctor

## KEY: MATCHING QUIZ/WORKSHEETS - *Treasure Island*

<u>Worksheet 1</u>
1. A
2. T
3. E
4. N
5. I
6. R
7. K
8. G
9. C
10. F
11. P
12. B
13. O
14. J
15. L
16. M
17. Q
18. H
19. S
20. D

<u>Worksheet 2</u>
1. C
2. D
3. R
4. I
5. G
6. P
7. M
8. N
9. T
10. L
11. B
12. A
13. Q
14. K
15. O
16. E
17. S
18. J
19. H
20. F

# JUGGLE LETTER REVIEW GAME CLUE Sheet - *Treasure Island*

| SCRAMBLED | WORD | CLUE |
| --- | --- | --- |
| ORANCH | ANCHOR | Jim cut the Hispaniola's |
| NEB | BEN | Man of the Island |
| WOBBEN | BENBOW | Admiral ____: the Hawkins' inn |
| LIBL | BILL | Told Jim to watch for a man with a wooden leg |
| KLADGOBC | BLACKDOG | Missing two fingers; saved by a wooden sign |
| SKOBLTAPC | BLACKSPOT | Death notice |
| SNOBE | BONES | Bill ____ |
| BLISROT | BRISTOL | Jim's home port |
| RACCELO | CORACLE | Ben's boat |
| EVOC | COVE | Protected waters |
| WREC | CREW | Those who work on the ship |
| TNILF | FLINT | Buried the treasure |
| NUG | GUN | The long nine was one |
| NUGN | GUNN | Ben ____ |
| THELMA | HAMLET | Jim & his mother went to the neighboring ___ |
| SHADN | HANDS | Israel ____ |
| SWINKAH | HAWKINS | Jim's last name |
| ANOSHPILAI | HISPANIOLA | Name of the ship that went to Treasure Island |
| NIDALS | ISLAND | Treasure _____ |
| SAIERL | ISRAEL | Jim killed him |
| MIJ | JIM | Boy narrator |
| LOORRELYGJ | JOLLY ROGER | Pirate flag |
| YEEVLIS | LIVESEY | Magistrate and doctor |
| PAM | MAP | Shows where the treasure is |
| SMAT | MAST | Tall pole on a ship |
| TAMES | MATES | Hands on a ship |
| INTUMY | MUTINY | When the mates overthrow the captain |
| HOOLLTIC | OILCLOTH | Contained the map |
| WPE | PEW | Blind buccaneer |
| TRAPIE | PIRATE | Buccaneer |
| TROP | PORT | Bristol, for example; city place where ships dock |
| TREDHUR | REDRUTH | First of Smollett's men to die |
| UMR | RUM | Pirates' drink |
| HIPS | SHIP | Big boat; sea transport |
| RIVELS | SILVER | Captain Long John ___ |

| | | |
|---|---|---|
| LOMSTELT | SMOLLETT | Capt. of ship going to Treasure Island |
| RQSEUI | SQUIRE | Trelawney; best shot of Smollett's group |
| NETNOSEVS | STEVENSON | Author |
| DESTCAKO | STOCKADE | Blockhouse where Smollett's men stayed for a while |
| OTSW | STOW | ___ away; hide |
| STEERRUA | TREASURE | _____ Island |
| CURTE | TRUCE | A white flag is a sign of this |
| NIEW | WINE | What Hands wanted Jim to get |

# VOCABULARY RESOURCE MATERIALS

# VOCABULARY WORD SEARCH - *Treasure Island*

All words in this list are associated with *Treasure Island* with an emphasis on the vocabulary words chosen for study in the text. The words are placed backwards, forward, diagonally, up and down. The included words are listed below.

```
V W F Z Q M C X R R F D X E V Y J B D P S B Z L
Z M M S U F Y I K B U O B H C Y T T L E I C B Q
P N Z T W R C L Z R T J L X E N E C V C L K E J
W A I N R O P E S K R A W L U B A V O W E D E D
Y N T A C E L T T A K V L P Y C F N A M U N I S
Y P T H W J T L L X B O J G H B N G G T R Z Y S
F D E G W S L S I P V R O E F O Q S I U S A K Y
R T O J D A T X A B E N E Y I T P L C E P S D Y
L R K L F E R A V M E R W S P N O A R O U E M E
G K C E D X S T O S R O S I H S K U L O U P R X
H L B A H R E P D B L E R O T E T L I I C R T C
C W O U N L U Z E L U C T E N X A U I O S J L M
F O M O C N M M A R S H B R I A Q R N N R A U R
R Y X A P C I T S E A B I M A E G S K C G T D Y
K U R W R H A K D C I D D T S U O E A E O S R E
N O F D A O O N I G O A O B H R Q P R T N U L M
C X R F B I O L E N M G O E T E S N E H J I T T
P H G D I N N E E Y K N G S T R E Y R B Y N H
W X D D X A M D E Z R S H A A Z T T E S G G K G
F A R T H I N G Q D W S G N C F A P O P L E X Y
```

| | | | |
|---|---|---|---|
| ADMIXTURE | COMRADE | INKLING | SABRE |
| APOPLEXY | CONNOISSEUR | LOOPHOLE | SCOUR |
| ATHWART | CONSORT | MAROONED | SIDLED |
| AVOWED | CORACLE | MUTINY | SOLITUDE |
| BEFALL | COXWAIN | NONDESCRIPT | STAVE |
| BILLOWS | DESPERADOES | OBSEQUIOUS | TALLOWY |
| BOATSWAIN | DOLDRUMS | PALISADE | TARRY |
| BUCCANEERS | DURST | PERJURY | TEETOTUM |
| BULWARKS | FARTHING | PERSONAGE | UNCOUTH |
| BYGONES | FOLLY | PIKES | VOLLEY |
| CACHE | GIBBET | QUARTERMASTER | WAINROPES |
| CANNIKIN | GROG | REPUGNANCE | |
| CAPSTAN | HEARKENING | RICOCHET | |
| COGNAC | HITHERTO | RUFFIAN | |

# VOCABULARY CROSSWORD *Treasure Island*

# VOCABULARY CROSSWORD CLUES - *Treasure Island*

## ACROSS

3. Great waves or surges of water
8. A stroke caused by a rupture of an artery of the brain
9. Insubordination; refusal to obey orders
10. Unhappy
11. Kind of gallows on which malefactors were hung in chains and allowed to remain there as a warning
12. Hands on a ship
13. Foolishness
14. Small can or drinking vessel
16. Color of blood
17. Dared
19. Warns
20. Spears
23. In opposition to; across the length, direction or course of
24. Hole in the ground used as a hiding place
26. Simultaneous discharge of arrows, bullets, etc.
29. To move swiftly on foot
30. Number of years in existence
31. Protected waters
32. The long nine was one
35. Big boat; sea transport
38. Linger or delay
39. Pirates
42. Left in hopeless isolation
43. Narrow strips to form the sides of a barrel; to break a hole in; to ward off
44. Opposite of above
45. Israel ____
46. Tall pole on a ship
50. Muskets; firearms
51. Act of complying passively without implying agreement

## DOWN

1. Officer on a ship in charge of rigging & cables
2. Man of the Island
3. Past; things gone by
4. Propel in a high arc
5. Standing in the rain or swimming one gets ---
6. Moved sideways
7. Declared openly
8. That which is added to anything by mixing
9. Belonging to me
10. To make clean & bright by friction; to clear away; diarrhea in cattle
13. British bronze coin worth one fourth of a penny
14. A boat made by covering a wicker frame with hide or cloth
15. A hint; a slight knowledge or vague notion
18. Unrefined
21. A cavalry sword with a somewhat curved blade
22. Any intoxicating liquor
25. A superior French brandy
27. A small opening through which small arms may be discharged
28. A mate; companion; associate
33. A fence of pales or stakes for defense; a line of bold cliffs
34. Those who work on the ship
36. A ship keeping company with another
37. A child's toy somewhat like a top
39. To happen to
40. A kind of pulley
41. Look
42. Shows where the treasure is
47. Sound of a clock ---- tock
48. Pirates' drink
49. Blind buccaneer

# VOCABULARY CROSSWORD *Treasure Island*

# VOCABULARY WORKSHEET 1 - *Treasure Island*

____ 1. State of being alone; seclusion
    A. Pikes    B. Farthing    C. Solitude    D. Tallowy

____ 2. Small can or drinking vessel
    A. Obsequious    B. Desperadoes    C. Hearkening    D. Cannikin

____ 3. Muskets; firearms
    A. Undulating    B. Cognac    C. Consort    D. Musketry

____ 4. Declared openly
    A. Inkling    B. Avowed    C. Marooned    D. Coracle

____ 5. A stroke caused by a rupture of an artery of the brain
    A. Apoplexy    B. Billows    C. Tallowy    D. Coracle

____ 6. To make clean & bright by friction; to clear away; diarrhea in cattle
    A. Loophole    B. Reverberations    C. Marooned    D. Scour

____ 7. One competent to act as a critical judge of an art or in a matter of taste
    A. Connoisseur    B. Musketry    C. Obsequious    D. Doldrums

____ 8. To happen to
    A. Loophole    B. Befall    C. Obsequious    D. Stave

____ 9. A cruel, brutal person
    A. Capstan    B. Quartermaster    C. Ruffian    D. Athwart

____ 10. British bronze coin worth one fourth of a penny
    A. Coxwain    B. Sabre    C. Farthing    D. Uncouth

____ 11. False swearing; voluntary violation of an oath
    A. Palisade    B. Perjury    C. Coxwain    D. Farthing

____ 12. Hole in the ground used as a hiding place
    A. Cache    B. Uncouth    C. Mutiny    D. Gibbet

____ 13. A mate; companion; associate
    A. Comrade    B. Nondescript    C. Grog    D. Doldrums

____ 14. Linger or delay
    A. Sidled    B. Hitherto    C. Tarry    D. Pikes

____ 15. Narrow strips to form the sides of a barrel; to break a hole in; to ward off
    A. Farthing    B. Musketry    C. Stave    D. Pike

____ 16. Side of a ship above the upper deck; any strong safeguards
    A. Bulwarks    B. Desperadoes    C. Doldrums    D. Folly

____ 17. Officer who provides quarters, clothing, etc. for troops
    A. Quartermaster    B. Athwart    C. Consort    D. Apoplexy

____ 18. Until now
    A. Palisade    B. Hitherto    C. Volley    D. Marooned

____ 19. That which is added to anything by mixing
    A. Admixture    B. Personage    C. Doldrums    D. Musketry

____ 20. Unrefined
    A. Cognac    B. Nondescript    C. Mutiny    D. Uncouth

# VOCABULARY WORKSHEET 2 - *Treasure Island*

____ 1. COXWAIN

____ 2. TARRY

____ 3. TEETOTUM

____ 4. CACHE

____ 5. BEFALL

____ 6. CANNIKIN

____ 7. TALLOWY

____ 8. GROG

____ 9. UNCOUTH

____ 10. APOPLEXY

____ 11. LOOPHOLE

____ 12. AVOWED

____ 13. MAROONED

____ 14. ATHWART

____ 15. SIDLED

____ 16. CONSORT

____ 17. BILLOWS

____ 18. ADMIXTURE

____ 19. GIBBET

____ 20. CAPSTAN

A. In opposition to; across the length, direction or course of

B. Moved sideways

C. Unrefined

D. A stroke caused by a rupture of an artery of the brain

E. Hole in the ground used as a hiding place

F. A child's toy somewhat like a top

G. A kind of pulley

H. A small opening through which small arms may be discharged

I. Left in hopeless isolation

J. Linger or delay

K. A ship keeping company with another

L. That which is added to anything by mixing

M. Great waves or surges of water

N. Pertaining to the fat of beef or mutton which has been extracted by melting

O. Any intoxicating liquor

P. Kind of gallows on which malefactors were hung in chains and allowed to remain there as a warning

Q. Small can or drinking vessel

R. To happen to

S. Declared openly

T. Steersman of a ship's boat

# KEY: VOCABULARY WORKSHEETS - *Treasure Island*

| Worksheet 1 | Worksheet 2 |
|---|---|
| 1. C | 1. T |
| 2. D | 2. J |
| 3. D | 3. F |
| 4. B | 4. E |
| 5. A | 5. R |
| 6. D | 6. Q |
| 7. A | 7. N |
| 8. B | 8. O |
| 9. C | 9. C |
| 10. C | 10. D |
| 11. B | 11. H |
| 12. A | 12. S |
| 13. A | 13. I |
| 14. C | 14. A |
| 15. C | 15. B |
| 16. A | 16. K |
| 17. A | 17. M |
| 18. B | 18. L |
| 19. A | 19. P |
| 20. D | 20. G |

## VOCABULARY JUGGLE LETTER REVIEW GAME CLUES - *Treasure Island*

| SCRAMBLED | WORD | CLUE |
|---|---|---|
| UCQAECINEECS | ACQUIESCENCE | Act of complying passively without implying agreement |
| IRUTXMEDA | ADMIXTURE | That which is added to anything by mixing |
| PAXPOYLE | APOPLEXY | A stroke caused by a rupture of an artery of the brain |
| HARWATT | ATHWART | In opposition to; across the length, direction or course of |
| WDVOEA | AVOWED | Declared openly |
| LBEAFL | BEFALL | To happen to |
| LIBLWOS | BILLOWS | Great waves or surges of water |
| TSWNOBAIA | BOATSWAIN | Officer on a ship in charge of rigging & cables |
| CUBANRECSE | BUCCANEERS | Pirates |
| SRULBWAK | BULWARKS | Side of a ship above the upper deck; any strong safeguards |
| GNEOYBS | BYGONES | Past; things gone by |
| HEACC | CACHE | Hole in the ground used as a hiding place |
| KINIACNN | CANNIKIN | Small can or drinking vessel |
| PCSANTA | CAPSTAN | A kind of pulley |
| ONCGAC | COGNAC | A superior French brandy |
| ERADCMO | COMRADE | A mate; companion; associate |
| SOSURENCONI | CONNOISSEUR | One competent to act as a critical judge of an art or in a matter of taste |
| TSROCNO | CONSORT | A ship keeping company with another |
| OEALRCC | CORACLE | A boat made by covering a wicker frame with hide or cloth |
| XINAWCO | COXWAIN | Steersman of a ship's boat |
| EEDDSSEOPAR | DESPERADOES | Desperate criminals |
| UDLODMRS | DOLDRUMS | Part of the ocean near the equator abounding in calms, squalls, and baffling winds |
| TUDSR | DURST | Dared |
| NTIGHFRA | FARTHING | British bronze coin worth one fourth of a penny |
| LFOYL | FOLLY | Foolishness |
| BETBIG | GIBBET | Kind of gallows on which malefactors were hung in chains and allowed to remain there as a warning |
| ORGG | GROG | Any intoxicating liquor |
| RGKNEIENAH | HEARKENING | Listening |
| IHRTOTHE | HITHERTO | Until now |
| GKINLIN | INKLING | A hint; a slight knowledge or vague notion |
| POLOLOHE | LOOPHOLE | A small opening through which small arms may be discharged |

| | | |
|---|---|---|
| ONORMAED | MAROONED | Left in hopeless isolation |
| UKESMYRT | MUSKETRY | Muskets; firearms |
| IUYMNT | MUTINY | Insubordination; refusal to obey orders |
| TONNSEDPIRC | NONDESCRIPT | Not easily described; of no particular class or kind |
| QUUOOSSEBI | OBSEQUIOUS | Fawning; obedient; compliant |
| EPLADIAS | PALISADE | A fence of pales or stakes for defense; a line of bold cliffs |
| EPRRYUJ | PERJURY | False swearing; voluntary violation of an oath |
| GEPRENSOA | PERSONAGE | A person of distinction |
| SKEIP | PIKES | Spears |
| CNENAERGPU | REPUGNANCE | Aversion; loathing; disdain |
| IRCTEHCO | RICOCHET | To skip with a glancing rebound or series of rebounds |
| IFRUFNA | RUFFIAN | A cruel, brutal person |
| ERSAB | SABRE | A cavalry sword with a somewhat curved blade |
| RCUOS | SCOUR | To make clean & bright by friction; to clear away; diarrhea in cattle |
| DLSIDE | SIDLED | Moved sideways |
| EDSLOIUT | SOLITUDE | State of being alone; seclusion |
| VTESA | STAVE | Narrow strips to form the sides of a barrel; to break a hole in; to ward off |
| LYOLTWA | TALLOWY | Pertaining to the fat of beef or mutton which has been extracted by melting |
| RTYRA | TARRY | Linger or delay |
| OETUMETT | TEETOTUM | A child's toy somewhat like a top |
| OUHTNUC | UNCOUTH | Unrefined |
| NTNULUDIGA | UNDULATING | Moving up and down or backward and forward |
| LOVELY | VOLLEY | Simultaneous discharge of arrows, bullets, etc. |
| IWSEPRONA | WAINROPES | A cart rope; a trace or part of a harness |

www.ingramcontent.com/pod-product-compliance
Lightning Source LLC
Chambersburg PA
CBHW051418070526
44584CB00023B/3474